The New CAMBRIDGE English Course

PRACTICE

1

MICHAEL SWAN
CATHERINE WALTER

CAMBRIDGE
UNIVERSITY PRESS

Published by the Press Syndicate of the University of Cambridge
The Pitt Building, Trumpington Street, Cambridge CB2 1RP
40 West 20th Street, New York, NY 10011–4211, USA
10 Stamford Road, Oakleigh, Melbourne 3166, Australia

© Michael Swan and Catherine Walter 1990

First Published 1990
Ninth printing 1993

Designed by Banks and Miles, London
Cover design by Michael Peters & Partners Limited, London
Typeset by Wyvern Typesetting, Bristol
Printed in Great Britain by The Bath Press, Avon

ISBN 0 521 37649 1 Practice Book 1

Practice Book 1 split edition:
ISBN 0 521 37653 X Practice Book 1A
ISBN 0 521 37654 8 Practice Book 1B

ISBN 0 521 37661 0 Practice Book 1 with Key

ISBN 0 521 37637 8 Student's Book 1

Student's Book 1 split edition:
ISBN 0 521 37641 6 Student's Book 1A
ISBN 0 521 37642 4 Student's Book 1B

ISBN 0 521 37665 3 Teacher's Book 1

ISBN 0 521 37669 6 Test Book 1

ISBN 0 521 37502 9 Class Cassette Set 1

ISBN 0 521 37506 1 Student's Cassette Set 1

Student's Cassettes 1 split edition:
ISBN 0 521 38222 X Student's Cassette 1A
ISBN 0 521 38223 8 Student's Cassette 1B

ISBN 0 521 42728 2 Video 1 (VHS PAL)
ISBN 0 521 42729 0 Video 1 (VHS SECAM)
ISBN 0 521 42730 4 Video 1 (VHS NTSC)
ISBN 0 521 42731 2 Video Teacher's Guide 1
ISBN 0 521 44704 6 Video Teacher's Guide 1 without photocopiable tasks
ISBN 0 521 44703 8 Video Student's Activity Book 1

Contents

Unit 1 Hello

1A What's your name?

1 Write the sentences.

1. What's your name?

2. Carmen. What's your name?

3. Is your name Joe?

4. No, it isn's. It's Matija.

5. Is your name Lucy?

6. Yes, it is.

7. Is your name Sally?

8. Yes, it is.

9. Hello. My name's Anne.

10. My name Lula?

2 Write the full forms.

1. No, it *isn't*. No, it is not.
2. *What's* your name?
3. My *name's* Judy.
4. *It's* Mary.

3 Write the answers.

1. One + one = two
2. Three − two = one
3. Two + one = three
4. Three − one = two
5. One + two = three

4 Pronounce these.

isn't   it isn't   No, it isn't.
name   your name   What's your name?
is   it is   Yes, it is.

5 Translate these into your language.

1. Hello. My name's Mary Lake.
2. Hello. Yes, room three one two, Mrs Lake.
3. Thank you.

4. What's your name?
5. Catherine.
6. What's *your* name?
7. John.

8. Is your name Mark Perkins?
9. No, it isn't. It's Harry Brown.

6 If you have Student's Cassette A, find Unit 1, Lesson A, Exercise 1. Listen and try to write the conversations. Check with Student's Book Exercise 1. Say the sentences.

1

2

1B His name's James Wharton

1 Complete the sentences with *my* or *your*.

1. What's *your* name?
2. Hello. *My* name's Bond – James Bond.
3. 'Is *your* name Anne?' 'Yes, that's right.'
4. '*My* name's Robert, isn't it?' 'No, it's Mike.'

2 Complete the sentences with *his* or *her*.

1. *My* name's Brigitte.
2. *My* name's James.
3. 'Her name's Anne.' 'What's *your* surname?'
4. '*My* name's Lee.' 'Is that his first name or his surname?'

3 First name or surname?

1. Denise *first name*
2. Gavin
3. Quinton
4. Wharton
5. Dorrington
6. Gillian
7. Jowitt
8. James

4 Translate these into your language.

1. Her name.
2. His name.
3. Her surname is Quinton.
4. His first name is James.
5. I don't know.
6. Yes, that's right.
7. No, it isn't.

5 Crossword puzzle.

ACROSS

2. *What*'s your name?
3. *My* name's Jacqueline Onassis.
6. 'Is *your* name Paul?' 'Yes, it is.'
7. Not *her*.
8. Yes, *it* is.

DOWN

1. What's your *name*?
4. Yes, that's *right*.
5. Not *yes*.
6. Not *no*.

(Solution on page 130.)

6 If you have Student's Cassette A, find Unit 1, Lesson B, Exercise 5. Listen and repeat.

1   2

"Right! What's your name?"

5

1C How are you?

1 Write the answers.

1. 'Hello.' '_Hello_,'
2. 'How are you?' 'I'm _happy_,'
3. 'What's your name?' '_Marjio_,'
4. 'How do you do?' '_I'm fine, and you_?'

2 Complete the conversations.

'Excuse _me_. Is _your_ name Alice Stevens?'
'No, _I'm_ sorry. _My name's_ Alice Carter.'

* * *

Excuse me. _Are_ you Bill Wallace?'
'_Yes_, I'_m_.'
'Hello, Bill. _My_ name's Jane Marks.'

3 Write the answers.

1. Six ÷ three = _two_
2. Six ÷ two = _three_
3. Three + two = _five_
4. Five − one = _four_
5. Five − three = _two_
6. One × five = _five_
7. One + one + two = _four_
8. (Two + three + one) ÷ two = _three_
9. Four − three = _one_
10. Four − two + four = _six_

4 *Excuse me* or *I'm sorry*?

1 _Excuse me_

2 _I'm sorry_

3 _I'm sorry_   4 _Excuse me_   5 _I'm sorry_

5 Translate these into your language.

1. Hello.
2. How are you?
3. How do you do?
4. Fine, thanks.
5. Excuse me.
6. I'm sorry.

1D Where are you from?

1 Read these words with the correct stress.

Australia	Australian
Germany	German
England	English
Britain	British
Italy	Italian
China	Chinese
Japan	Japanese

2 Write the full forms.

1. *I'm* English. _I am English_
2. No, it *isn't*. _No, it isn't it_
3. *He's* from Tanzania. _He is from Tanzania_
4. *She's* American. _She is American_
5. *I'm* from Oxford. _I am from Oxford_
6. *Where's* she from? _Wher is she from._

STOWELL

3 Put the adjectives with the right pictures.

Thai   French   Japanese
Cuban   Swiss   British
Egyptian   Chinese   Greek
German

1. Swiss
chocolate

2. a Thai
dancer

3. an Egyptian
pyramid

4. a Japanese
camera

5. a Greek
statue

6. a German
car

7. a British
car

8. French
perfume

9. a Cuban
cigar

10. a Chinese
plate

4 Translate these into your language.

1. Where are you from?
2. She's from India.
3. He's Chinese.
4. Helena's from Greece.
5. Andrew's Scottish.

5 If you have Student's Cassette A, find Unit 1, Lesson D, Exercise 4. Say the words from Student's Book Exercise 4, and check your pronunciation with the tape.

1   2

6 Crossword puzzle.

ACROSS

1. She's English. She's from England
3. 'What's your name?' 'Jowitt.'
5. wher are you from?
6. Andrew is Scotish. He's from Scotland.
9. She's French. Her name's Isabelle.
10. 6.
11. 'Is your name Catherine?' 'Yes, it is.'
12. Yumiko is from Tokyo. She's Japanese
15. Tony's from Australia. He's Australian
17. She's from India. She's Indian.
19. 'Are you American?' 'Yes, I am.'
20. He's from England. His name's Mark Perkins.
22. 'Where is Anne from?' 'I don't know.'
23. 3.
24. 5.

DOWN

1. Excuse me. Are you Gavin Jowitt?
2. Sharon's from the United States. She's American
4. isn't = is not
6. Carlos is from Madrid. He's Spanish
7. Colette's Swiss. She is from Zurich.
8. Erik's German. he is from Germany.
13. I speak Spanish, French, and a little English.
14. Where are you from?
16. 2.
17. 'Is his surname Hayashi?' 'Yes, it is.'
18. 'What's her name?' 'I'm sorry, I don't know.'
21. 'Is Carla from Rome?' 'Yes, She is.'

(Solution on page 130.)

Unit 2 You

2A What do you do?

1 Put in *I, you, he, she, it, my, your, his* or *her.*

1. 'Are _you_ Mary Lewis?' 'Yes, _I_ am.'
2. She's from Spain. _Her_ name's Carmen.
3. _he_'s from Japan. His name's Mr Watanabe.
4. 'Are _you_ Italian?' 'No, I'm Greek.'
5. 'Is your name John Collett?' 'No, _it_ isn't.'
6. _My_ name's Alice Stephens. I'm a dentist.

2 Say these words with the correct stress.

artist	dentist	United
electrician	surname	Excuse me
engineer	Hello	Chinese
architect	Goodbye	British

3 Add some more words to these lists.

A	AN
a doctor	an electrician
a house	an apartment

4 Complete the dialogues.

A: _What's your name_ ?
B: It's Smith.
A: _Okay_., Mr Smith?
B: James.
A: _____?
B: I'm an electrician.

A: _Are you a_ photographer?
B: No, _I'm an_ accountant.
A: Oh!

A: _You are a_ doctor?
B: No, _I'm an_ actress.

A: _You are a_ pilot?
B: Yes, _It is_.

5 Translate these into your language.

1. What do you do?
2. How do you do?
3. How are you?
4. I'm an engineer.
5. She's an engineer.
6. He's an engineer.
7. Is she a doctor?
8. Yes, she is.
9. No, she isn't.

6 If you have Student's Cassette A, find Unit 2, Lesson A, Exercise 5. Say the words from Student's Book Exercise 5, and check your pronunciation with the tape.

1   2

2B I'm very well, thank you

1 Put in *am, 'm not, are(n't), 's* or *isn't*.

1. Hello. How _are_ you?
2. How _aren't_ your daughter today?
3. 'Are you English?' 'Yes, I _are_.'
4. 'Judith _aren't_ a doctor.' 'No, she
   _............_. She's a dentist.'
5. 'Are you an artist?' 'No, I _............_'

2 Morning, afternoon, evening or night?

1 _morning or evening_   2   3

4   5   6

3 Complete the dialogues.

Dialogue 1
A: _............_?
B: Not bad. And you?
A: _............_.

Dialogue 2
A: _............_?
B: Good afternoon, Mr Kowalski. I'm fine, thank you. And you?
A: _............_.

Dialogue 3
A: Hello. I'm Polly. What's your name?
B: _............_.
   _............_?
A: No, I'm Australian. And you?
B: _............_.
   _............_ teacher?
A: Yes, I am. Oh, dear! It's 10.45! I must go. Bye!
B: _............_.

4 Put the words from the boxes into lists.

artist	Chinese	doctor	electrician
engineer	he	her	his	housewife	Italian
John	Mary	photographer	secretary	she
shop assistant	Spanish	student	Susan
Tom

WOMAN	MAN	WOMAN OR MAN
Mary	John	artist

5 Copy and complete the table.

| I am (_............_) |
| you _............_ (you're) |
| he/_............_/it is (_............_) |

| _............_ I? |
| are you? |
| _............_? |

| I am not (_............_) |
| you _............_ (you aren't) |
| he/she/it _............_ (_............_) |

6 Translate these into your language.

1. Good morning.
2. Hello.
3. Good afternoon.
4. Good evening.
5. I'm very well, thank you.
6. Fine, thanks.
7. I'm not well today.
8. Oh, I'm sorry to hear that.

7 If you have Student's Cassette A, find Unit 2, Lesson B, Exercise 2. Say the conversations in Student's Book Exercise 2, and check your pronunciation with the tape.

Good morning, Mr Roberts. Good morning, Mr Roberts.

1   2

2C I'm an actress. And you?

1 Put in *I, you, he, she, am, 'm, are, 're, is* or *'s.*

1. George is Swiss. .... is from Geneva.
2. 'Mrs Alexander isn't English.' 'No? Where's .... from?'
3. 'Are you American?' 'Yes, I ....'
4. 'What do .... do?' '...............'m a doctor.'
5. '............... you married?' 'Yes, I ....'
6. 'What............... your name?' 'Charles.'
7. '............... your name Alice?' 'No, it ....n't.'
8. 'What does Mary do?' '............... .... a shop assistant.'

2 Write the questions.

1. '...............?' 'No, I'm single.'
2. ' *What do you do* ?' 'I'm a doctor.'
3. '...............?' 'Australia.'
4. '...............?' 'John Cagney.'
5. '...............?' 'No, it's Mary.'

3 Put in the missing words.

1. 'Are you Italian?' 'No, I'm .... France.'
2. I .... a little Portuguese.
3. 'What's your ....?' 'Michael.' 'And your ....?' 'Smith.'
4. Excuse ....
5. '............... are you?' 'Fine, ...'

4 First name or surname?

| Alice Anne Barker Bill Catherine |
| Dan Jackson James Jane Jennings |
| John Manning Mary Miriam Perkins |
| Peter Philip Sarah Steve Susan Tom |
| Wagner Watson Webber Wharton |

First name   Surname
Alice   Barker

5 Translate these into your language.

1. eleven
2. twelve
3. thirteen
4. nineteen
5. She's married.
6. He's single.
7. That's interesting.

6 If you have Student's Cassette A, find Unit 2, Lesson C, Exercise 1. Listen and practise. Note:

| thir**teen** | four**teen** | fif**teen** | six**teen** |
| seven**teen** | eigh**teen** | nine**teen** | |

1   2

7 Separate the two stories.

Alice is sixteen.
Steve is twenty.
His surname is Berczuk; it's a Ukrainian name.
She is a student from Aberdeen, in Scotland.
Her surname is MacAllen.
He's an artist, so his job is interesting.
He is from Australia, but now he is both British and Australian.
MacAllen is a Scottish name, not an English name.
Alice lives at 6 Menzies Way.
He is from Sydney.
His address in London is 113 Beech Road, NW2.
She is not very well today.

Alice	Steve
Alice is sixteen.	Steve is twenty. H

"Me?"

2D How old are you?

1 Correct these sentences.

1. whats your name
   <u>What's your name ?</u>
2. how old are you
3. im an engineer
4. suzanne is french
5. are you an architect
6. john isnt in england
7. shes twenty seven

2 Match words and numbers.

55	five	6	sixty-six	99	ninety
15	fifty-five	16	six	90	nineteen
50	fifty	60	sixteen	19	nine
5	fifteen	66	sixty	9	ninety-nine

3 Write these numbers in words. Example:

76 <u>seventy-six</u>

82	23	14	30	61
47	88	17	54	12

4 Which one is different?

1. morning   evening   night   (name)
2. Hi   How   Where   What
3. Italian   British   Japan   American
4. Hi.   Thanks.   Hello.   Good morning.
5. fine   very well   not bad   good
6. two   twenty-eight   seven   sixteen   six
7. eighty-two   five   thirty   ninety-five   ten

5 Complete the dialogue.

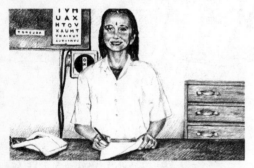

'Good morning. I'm Ms Wharton. Do sit down.
   Now, what's your name, please?'
'....................,'

'And your address?'
'....................,'

'Is that a London address?'
'....................,'

'I see. Now, how old are you, please?'
'....................,'

'And what's your job?'
'....................,'

'Fine. Now, how are you today?'
'....................,'

'OK. Please read this . . .'

6 Translate these into your language.

1. How old are you?
2. How are you?
3. He's separated.
4. She's divorced.
5. She's a widow.
6. a hundred
7. Mr Jackson
8. Mrs Jackson
9. Miss Jackson
10. Dr Jackson

7 If you have Student's Cassette A, find Unit 2, Lesson D, Exercise 1. Read the numbers from Student's Book Exercise 1, and check your pronunciation with the tape.

1   2

8 📼 Read this with a dictionary.

IT'S A LONG STORY
1

Judy Parker is twenty-two. She is a medical student. Judy is intelligent and very pretty, with a good sense of humour. She is a nice woman. Her boyfriend's name is Sam Watson. Sam is twenty-seven. He works in a bank as assistant manager. He is good-looking, but he is not a very nice man. Judy loves Sam very much. Sam loves money, cars, good food, whisky, travel and beautiful women.

📼 *This symbol means that a recording of this episode of It's a Long Story is on one of the Student's Cassettes.*

Unit 3 People

3A Andrew's bag's under the table

1 Rewrite the sentences as in the examples.

1. Where is Ann's hat? _Where is her hat?_
2. Dan's an architect. _Dan is an architect._
3. Ann's married.
4. John's bag is under the table.
5. Is Susan's book French?
6. Tom's pen isn't on the table.
7. Harry's coat's on the chair.
8. Mary's single.
9. Where's Alice's pen?
10. Dan's Italian.

2 Write questions.

1. Fine, thanks. _How are you?_
2. It's under the table. _Where's John's pen?_
3. How do you do?
4. I'm an engineer.
5. It's on the chair.
6. No, he isn't. He's a teacher.
7. No, it isn't. It's under my coat.
8. I'm very well, thank you.
9. No, I'm divorced.
10. She's not well today.
11. 17 Church Lane.
12. Q, U, I, N, T, O, N.
13. The United States.

3 Write labels for the pictures.

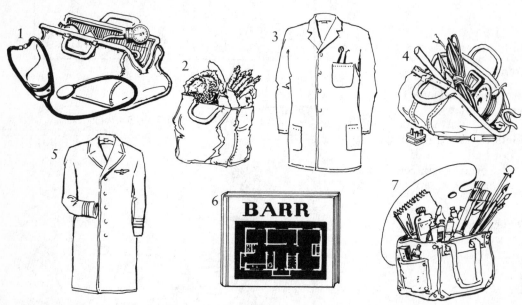

| an architect's book | an artist's bag | a dentist's coat | a pilot's coat |
| a doctor's bag | an electrician's bag | a housewife's bag | |

4 Write the answers.

1. What's your surname?
2. What's your first name?
3. What's your nationality?
4. How old are you?
5. Are you an architect?
6. Are you married?
7. How are you today?
8. Where's your bag?
9. Where's your Practice Book?

5 Translate these into your language.

1. John's coat is on the table.
2. Where's Polly's bag?
3. Is Ann's coat on the chair?
4. Ann's pen is on John's book.

6 If you have Student's Cassette A, find Unit 2, Lesson B, Exercise 2. Listen and try to write the conversations. Check with Student's Book Unit 2, Lesson B, Exercise 2.

Good morning, Mr Roberts.

3B This is Judy

1 Copy and complete the table.

I	am
you	....
he/she/it	....
we	....
you	....
....	are

2 Change the sentences. Use a dictionary.

1. My friend Alice and I are tall.
   We are tall.
2. Eric and George are very good-looking.
   They ...
3. Susan is a doctor.
4. My father and I are fair.
5. My children are quite intelligent.
6. Eric is very slim.
7. Andrew is not very tall.
8. Joan and Philip are tall and dark.
9. Mr and Mrs Carter are American.
10. John and I are quite good-looking.
11. You and your brother are engineers, aren't you?

3 Make questions. Use a dictionary.

1. your friend | a policeman
   Is your friend a policeman?
2. they | American
   Are ...
3. his father | English
4. Alice | married
5. you and your wife | British
6. John and Polly | doctors
7. Susan | pretty
8. Eric's girlfriend | tall
9. your secretary | good-looking
10. Ingrid and Christiane | German
11. your name | Sam Lewis
12. your boyfriend's name | Peter

4 Translate these into your language.

1. She is very pretty.
2. He is quite good-looking.
3. This is Sam's friend, Eric.
4. This is Sam's girlfriend, Judy.
5. 'She's English.' 'No, she's not. She's French.'

5 Cut pictures out of magazines and write about the people.

She's tall and fair

3C I've got three children

1 Put in *his, her, their, is* or *are*.

1. Monica and ..her.. mother ..are.. both doctors.
2. Philippe ..is.. French, and ..his.. wife .... German.
3. Joyce Price .... a photographer, and .... brother .... an accountant.
4. My sister and I .... American, but our grandparents .... Greek.
5. Sonia .... a doctor, and .... mother is a doctor too.
6. Henry's mother .... a shop assistant. .... name is Lucy.
7. George and Karen .... British; .... daughter .... married to an American.
8. Alice and Bill .... doctors, and .... son is a medical student.
9. What .... your brother's name?
10. 'John and Matthew .... brothers.' 'What .... surname?'

2 Pronounce:

John's   Mark's   Joyce's   Ann's   Alan's   Ronald's
Greece's   an artist's   Alice's   Mr Nash's   my parents'

3 Change the sentences as in the example.
Example:

Joyce has got a son. He is fourteen.

Joyce's son is fourteen

1. Peter has got a sister. She is very pretty.
2. My mother has got a brother. He is a doctor.
3. Anne has got a boyfriend. He is tall and good-looking.
4. Robert has got a girlfriend. She is not very pretty.
5. Mrs Lewis has got children. They are students.

4 Write five sentences about your family.

5 Write the plurals.

1. engineer _engineers_
2. boyfriend
3. artist
4. secretary
5. woman
6. doctor
7. child
8. country
9. daughter
10. man

6 Translate these into your language.

1. Joe and Ann have got three children.
2. I've got two daughters and a son.
3. What are their names?
4. My son's name is Fred.
5. My daughters' names are Alice and Lucy.
6. Who is John's daughter?

3D An interview

1 Complete the sentences.

1. I have .... three children.
2. How many children .... you got?
3. My father .... got two sisters.
4. I haven't .... any sisters.
5. .... any brothers or sisters?

2 Complete the dialogue.

A: Good morning, Mrs Martin.
B: ....
A: Please sit down.
B: ....
A: ....?
B Thirty-three.
A ....?
B: Yes, I ....
A: What is ....'s name?
B: Alex.
A: And ....?
B: Thirty-two.
A: Have you got any ....?
B: Yes, ... A boy and a ....

(Phone rings)

A: .... me, Mrs Martin. Hello? Yes. Yes.
I'm ...., I .... know. No. Goodbye.
I'm ...., Mrs Martin. Now, you want to borrow some money.
B: Yes.

3 Translate these into your language.

1. Sit down, please.
2. You're Canadian, aren't you?
3. Excuse me a moment.
4. How many children have you got?
5. Pardon?

4 If you have Student's Cassette A, find Unit 3, Lesson D, Exercise 1. Listen to the recording and practise the sentences.

1   2

"Here's to you and me and your husband and my wife."

5 💿 Read this with a dictionary.

| IT'S A LONG STORY |
| 2 |

Judy is worried. She doesn't know where Sam is. The bank manager doesn't know where Sam is, either. He is very worried.

Sam is in Brazil, in a small town on the coast near Rio de Janeiro, with £50,000 of the bank's money. He is sitting in a bar near the beach, drinking a large martini and writing a letter to Judy.

Rio, Tuesday.

Darling Judy,
Well, here I am in Brazil. It's very warm here, and the sea is nice for swimming. The women here are very beautiful, and very, very friendly. But I miss you, Judy. Please come and stay with me in Brazil. Can you take the 13.25 flight from London to Rio on April 14th? I'll meet you at the airport.
All my love
Sam

6 Try this crossword.

ACROSS

C. 4 + 2.
E. Leonardo da Vinci was a poet, ... artist and an engineer.
G. 3 × 2 − 1.
I. 6 − 5 + 4 − 3 − 2 + 1.
J. *C across* × 3 + 2.
N. 'Is Karsten Danish?' 'Yes, ... is.'
O. 'Are your grandparents Italian?' 'No, ... not.'
Q. 1, 2, 3, 4, etc.
T. 'Is your name Mary?' 'Yes, ... is.'
U. Three threes.
V. I've got .... children: two girls and a boy.
Y. My mother's American. ....'s from California.
Z. I speak a little ....
BB. *G across* × 2.
CC. .... you married?
EE. Mother's brother.
FF. No, I'm ....
GG. .... she Japanese?
HH. Good morning, ... Harris.

D
O
W
N

A. 'Where are you from?' '...............?' 'Where are you from?'
B. I'm sorry, I .... know.
C. 10 − 3.
D. 'Is your name Bernard?' 'No, ... isn't.'
F. 'Are you married?' '..............., I'm not.'
G. *C down* − 3.
H. *G down* × 2.
J. Sonia is Alan and Peter's mother; Philip is .... father.
K. 'Are you Mr and Mrs Harris?' 'Yes, ... are.'
L. The same as *F down*.
M. Thank ....
P. 6 + 5.
R. Good morning. .... name is Henry Martin.
S. Alice is English. She's from ....
V. 'Sit down, please.' '............... you.'
W. She's tall, but .... husband is very short.
X. We are.
AA. .... down, please.
BB. ...., 4, 6, 8, 10.
DD. Mary and .... sister are very pretty.
EE. United States.

(Solution on page 130.)

15

Unit 4 Consolidation

4A Things to remember: Units 1, 2 and 3

1 Copy and complete Catherine's family tree.

GEORGE — ANN ....

JOE .... — MARY ....
my father

ERIC .... — CATHERINE *me!* LUCY .... TOM .... — ALICE *my brother's ....*

SUSAN .... PHILIP .... DAN ....

4 Make plurals.

1. student *students*
2. age
3. widow
4. man
5. woman
6. boyfriend
7. child
8. family
9. parent
10. sister
11. wife
12. address
13. housewife
14. secretary

5 Write the names of these numbers.

100	12	58	95
83	32	10	76
17	14	2	29
70	40	61	11

2 Write *Where, Who, What,* or *How.*

1. '................ are you?' 'Fine, thanks.'
2. ....'s your name?
3. .... is your mother from?
4. .... old is John?
5. '................'s your dentist?' 'Mr Phillips.'
6. '................ do you do?' '................ do you do?'
7. .... do you spell your surname?
8. '................ do you do?' 'I'm a shop assistant.'
9. '................'s my bag?' 'I'm sorry, I don't know.'
10. .... does *slim* mean?

3 *Excuse me, Pardon* or *I'm sorry?*

1
2
3
Straight on. Straight on.
4
5
6

16

6 Do the crossword.

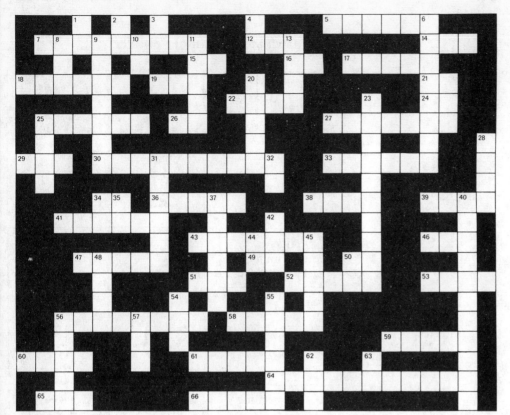

(Solution on page 130.)

ACROSS

5. .... sit down.
7. Morning, ..., evening, night.
12. .... down.
14. *isn't = is* ....
15. My hat is .... my bag.
16. '...............' 'Hello.'
17. Not old.
18. Parent; man.
19.
21. Not on, not under, not near.
22.
24. ...., I'm not.
25. Mother, father, sisters, brothers = ...
26. 'Is your name Harry?' 'No, ... isn't.'
27. Your mother's son = your ....
29. Child; boy.
30. Tom is Jane's boyfriend; Jane is Tom's ....
33. Your father's daughter = your ....
34. ...., here's my bus.
36.
38. 'What's his name?' 'I don't ....'
39. Not dark.
41. Mother or father.
43. I'm a medical ....

46.
47. Not on, not in, not near.
49. Not under, not in, not near.
50. You + I; or he + I; or she + I; or they + I.
51. Not young.
52. Plural of *wife*.
53. Not fair.
56. I've got a ....: what does *strong* mean?
58. I .... a little German.
59. 'Are you Italian?' 'Yes, that's ....'
60. Not fat.
61. 'How old is Alice?' '............... forty, I think.'
64. Job; it has got two Es, two Is, and two Cs in it.
65. 'Are you married?' '..............., I am.'
66.

DOWN

1. I, you, he, she, ..., we, you, they
2. Is 'Jennings' a first name .... a surname?
3. What .... you ....?
4. *What's = What* ....
6. A job.
8. Not slim.
9. Good ....
10. Not 'yes'.
11.

13. 'I'm an actress.' '...............'s interesting.'
20. Girl, boy, ..., man.
23. Plural of *housewife*.
25. Where are you ....?
28. One + one + two
31. A or B or C or D or E or F . . .
32. How .... you ....?
34. Is your child a girl .... a boy?
35. 'Is your brother a student?' 'No, ...'s a shop assistant.'
37. I speak a .... Spanish.
40. 'I'm a photographer.' 'That's ....'
42.
44. How .... you spell it?
45. 'How old is Dan?' 'About twenty-two, I ....'
48. First name + surname
50. *50 across*
54. Man, woman, ..., girl.
55. G or H or I or J or K or L . . .
56. Miriam is .... tall.
57. Alice is strong, and her daughter is very strong ....
62. My, your, his, ...
63. Is he fair .... dark?

17

4B Please write

1 Write the questions.

1. Spain. *Where are you from?*
2. It's near the table.
3. Not bad, thanks. And you?
4. I'm a housewife.
5. L, O, P, E, Z.
6. Lopez.
7. Teresa.
8. She's seven.
9. No, I'm sorry, it's not. It's Jake Barker.
10. How do you do?
11. Good night.
12. Yes, a girl and two boys.
13. No, they're dentists.

2 Find words for the blanks.

1. 'How old are you?' '.............. fifteen.'
2. 'Are you Japanese?' 'Yes, ...'
3. 'Is John an electrician?' 'Yes, ...'
4. .... surname is Brown.
5. .... student.
6. My sons are very ....
7. 'How old is Mickey Mouse?' 'He's
   .... fifty.'
8. Is Robin a man's name .... a woman's
   name?
9. 'I'm from Texas.' 'Oh! I'm from Texas,
   ....'
10. 'How do you spell your name, Polly?'
    'P, O, ..., Y.'

3 Stress. Complete the lists with words from the box. Can you add any words?

address	afternoon	brother	divorced
doctor	double	engineer	evening
excuse	family	goodbye	hello
housewife	husband	interesting	letter
little	married	morning	number
question	secretary	single	sister
sorry	student	surname	table
teacher	widow	woman	

☐☐   ☐☐   ☐☐☐
brother   address   family

doctor   divorced   interesting

☐☐☐
afternoon

Notice the stress in these words. Say them.

separated   intelligent   electrician   university

4 Match the words to the pictures.

tall
quite tall
very tall

intelligent
quite intelligent
very intelligent

Good evening.
Hi.
Good night.

It's Italy.
It's Italian.

in
near
on
under

fair
dark
slim
fat

18

5 Do you know these words? If not, look them up in the dictionary.

ex-   good   holiday   home   international   newspaper
page   player   swimmer   tennis court

Now put this text in the right order.

She's a journalist for the international page of a daily newspaper.
She's a dark, slim, pretty woman, and very intelligent.
My friend Solange is from Paris.
She speaks English, German, Spanish and a little Italian.

Her holiday home has got a swimming pool,
He is quite tall and fair, and a good swimmer.
she and her ex-husband have got one son, Julien.
and a good tennis player.
Solange is divorced;
and it is near a tennis court.
Solange is a good swimmer, too,
He is fifteen.

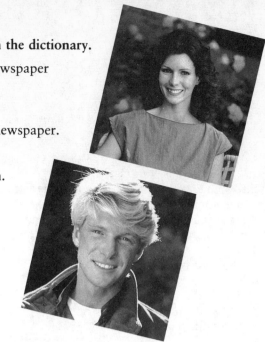

6 Look at the text about Solange, and write about your mother, father, wife, husband, boyfriend, girlfriend, brother, sister, teacher, boss . . .

4C I've got a new girlfriend

1 Copy and complete the table.

I	....	....	I'm	....	....	am I?
....	your	....	....	you are not	....	....
....	....	he is	....	....	he isn't	....
she	....	....	she's	....	....	is she?
....	(its)	....	....	it is not	....	....
....	our	we are	....	....	we aren't	....
....	....	you are	....	....	you aren't	....
they	....	....	they're	they are not	....	are they?

2 Write the full forms.

1. *Susan's* an engineer. <u>Susan is</u>
2. *They're* Italian.
3. *I've* got five brothers.
4. Dan and Catherine *aren't* in England.
5. They *haven't* got any children.
6. *He's* a photographer.
7. *How's* your daughter?
8. *John's* not very tall.
9. *What's* your name, please?
10. *I'm* quite tall.

3 *'s: is, his* or *her*?

1. John's pen is under your book. <u>his pen</u>
2. John's an electrician. <u>John is</u>
3. Susan's secretary isn't well. <u>her secretary</u>
4. Where's Ann's bag?
5. Are Dan's books in your bag?
6. I think Ann's about fifty.
7. Tom's English.
8. Is Tom's mother English?
9. I haven't got my daughter's coat.
10. My daughter's very pretty, and very intelligent.

4 's or s'?

1. Lucy has got a daughter. Her daughter is fair.
   Lucy's daughter is fair
2. My sons have got pens. The pens are in their bags.
   My sons' pens are in their bags
3. Eric has got a son. He is fourteen.
4. My daughters have got a teacher. She is Canadian.
5. My father has got a sister. She is an artist.
6. Alice has got a doctor. He is not very intelligent.
7. My students have got books. Their books are on the table.
8. Dr Wagner has got two brothers. They are doctors too.

5 Find words for the blanks.

1. 'How .... your name, Philip?'
   'P, H, I, L, I, P.'
2. Are you American .... Canadian?
3. My daughters are very ....
4. .... surname is Gomez.
5. .... engineer.
6. 'How old is James Bond?' 'I think he's .... thirty-five.'
7. 'My sister is a photographer.' 'That's interesting. My sister is a photographer, ...'
8. 'Is Alice an engineer?' 'Yes, ...'
9. 'How old is your mother?' '............... forty-three.'
10. 'Are you Italian?' 'Yes, ...'

6 Read the puzzle and answer the question.

Elizabeth, John, Harry, Mary and Tom are a family. The two doctors are fair. The father and the daughter are dark. Mary's children are an actress, an artist, and a doctor. Tom is an architect. Harry is dark. What is John's job?

(Solution on page 130.)

7 If you have Student's Cassette A, find Unit 4, Lesson C, Exercise 1. Listen to Andrew's part in the dialogue and try to remember Dan's part.

Hello, Dan. How are you?

Oh, hi, Andrew. Not bad, not bad.

1   2

8 ▣ Read this with a dictionary.

IT'S A LONG STORY
3

Judy is at home. (She lives in a small flat near the bank. It's not very nice.) She's in the living room, drinking a cup of coffee and thinking. Judy's very worried, because she doesn't know what to do. She loves Sam, and she doesn't want to tell the police where he is. But she doesn't want to go to Rio, either. She wants a quiet life.

Judy goes to the window and looks out. There's a police car in the street. Two big policemen are walking towards her house.

THERE IS NO PRACTICE BOOK WORK FOR LESSON 4D.

Unit 5 Where?

5A Home

1 Look at the picture and answer the questions.

1. Is there a table in the room?
   Yes, there is.
2. Are there any children in the room?
   Yes, there are three (children).
3. Is there a hat on the table?
   No, there isn't. There's a hat on the TV.
4. Are there any women in the room?
5. Is there a television near the table?
6. Are there any windows in the room?
7. Are there any books in the room?
8. Is there a cupboard in the room?
9. Is there a woman on the sofa?
10. Is there a man on the sofa?
11. Are there any bags under the table?
12. Are there any coats in the room?

2 Cut a picture of a room out of a magazine. Write five questions about the picture to give to another student.

3 Pronunciation. Underline the stressed syllables.

1. There are two bedrooms in the house.
2. There's a table in the living room.
3. There are three armchairs in the living room.
4. There's a woman on the sofa.
5. There are two children in the room.

4 *A/an* or *the*?

1. Look at .... picture on page 123.
2. There are five rooms in .... house.
3. There is .... armchair in .... living room.
4. There isn't .... garage.
5. There is .... fridge in .... kitchen.
6. My father is .... shop assistant.
7. He lives in .... flat in Manchester.

5 Read the information and write about the flats.

Jenny lives in a small flat and Sally lives in a big flat.

Jenny's flat

two rooms:
bed-sitting room   very small kitchen

and:
small bathroom with a shower and a toilet

in the kitchen:
small fridge

in the bed-sitting room:
black and white TV

Sally's flat

four rooms:
living room   two bedrooms   big kitchen

and:
bathroom   separate toilet

in the kitchen:
big fridge   dishwasher

in the living room:
colour TV

Write about Sally's flat by completing the following description.

There .... four .... in Sally's flat: a living room, two .... and a big
.... is .... bathroom too, and a separate .... In
the kitchen .... a big .... and a dishwasher. ....
.... colour .... in the ....

Now write about Jenny's flat.

6 Write about one of these: your house or flat, your 'dream house', or the house/flat of someone you know (your mother/brother/friend . . .).

7 *Believe it or not.* Read this with a dictionary.

There are only twelve letters in the Hawaiian alphabet: A, E, H, I, K, L, M, N, O, P,
    U and W.
There is a street in Canada that is 1,900km long.
There are about 790,000 words in English.
There are about 5,000 languages in the world (845 in India).
There are six different languages in Great Britain and Ireland (English, Welsh,
    Scots Gaelic, Irish Gaelic, Manx and Cornish).

5B Where do you work?

1 Put in the correct preposition (*at, in* or *on*).

1. I live .... 14 St Andrew's Place, Dundee.
2. My father lives .... a small house ....
   North London.
3. My girlfriend's flat is .... the seventh floor.
4. Do you live .... a house or a flat?
5. 'Where's the toilet, please?' '............... the second
   floor.'
6. 'Is there a doctor near here?' 'Yes, ... 37
   High Street.'
7. I lived .... America from 1976 to 1978.
8. She lives .... Pentonville Road.

2 *Live* or *lives*?

1. My Aunt Sally .... in New Jersey.
2. Where do you ....?
3. We .... at 141 Riverside Avenue, Cardiff.
4. My brother's wife .... in Chicago.
5. The Prime Minister .... at 10 Downing Street.

3 Say the names of these letters.

A   E   I   H   Y   R   K   W   G   Q
V   J   X   Z   U

Spell these words aloud.

address   age   John   eighteen   sorry
intelligent   night   interesting   Japan
housewife   evening   widow   married

Say these abbreviations.

USSR   TWA   BBC   EEC   USA   OK

4 Read this and fill in the table.

There are four floors in a block of flats. Two women and two men live in the flats; they are an architect, an artist, a doctor and a photographer. The architect lives on the ground floor. The photographer and the doctor are women. Philip is not an artist. Jane lives on the first floor. Susan is not a doctor; she lives under Dan.

NAME	JOB	FLOOR

(Solution on page 130.)

5 If you have Student's Cassette A, find Unit 5, Lesson B, Exercise 3 (only the first conversation is recorded here). Listen to the conversation and write down what the people say.

1   2

*"What do you mean other man? He's my husband.
You live next door."*

23

5C Where's the nearest post office?

1 Complete these dialogues.

A: ....?
B: Over there by the stairs.
A: ....

*   *   *

A: Excuse me. Where's Room 8, please?
B: ....
A: ....

*   *   *

A: Excuse me. Where's the nearest ....?
B: ....
A: ....

2 Answer these questions. Use *Yes, there is/are; No, there isn't/aren't* or *I don't know.*

1. Is there a bank in your street?
2. Is there a swimming pool near your home?
3. Is there an armchair in your bedroom?
4. Is there a television in your living room?
5. Is there a bus stop in your street?
6. Are there tigers in Canada?
7. Are there elephants in Thailand?
8. Are there penguins in Brazil?
9. Are there camels in India?
10. Is there a cat in your home?

3 True or false? Write *T* or *F* after each sentence. You can use your dictionary.

1. The USSR is 31 miles (50km) from the USA.
2. In 1710, there were 350 Europeans living in North America.
3. Mont Blanc is 6,000 metres high.
4. There are twenty pence (20p) in a pound sterling (£1).
5. There are a hundred cents (100¢) in a US dollar ($1).
6. There are three kilometres in a mile.
7. The President of the United States lives in the White House.
8. There are penguins in the Arctic.

(Answers on page 131.)

4 Make questions. Use *Is/Are there . . . ?*

1. lions | Uganda?   *Are there lions in Uganda ?*
2. an armchair | your bathroom?
3. a hotel | your street?
4. a bank | the station?
5. camels | Argentina?
6. a bus stop | this street?
7. a fridge | your kitchen?
8. crocodiles | Texas?

5 If you have Student's Cassette A, find Unit 5, Lesson C, Exercise 3. Play the conversation line by line and try to remember the next line. Check with Student's Book Exercise 3.

Excuse me. Where's the manager's office, please?

It's over there by the reception desk.

1   2

6 Read this with a dictionary.

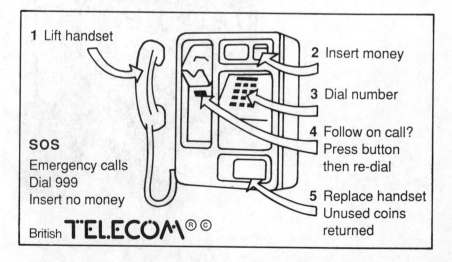

1 Lift handset

2 Insert money

3 Dial number

4 Follow on call? Press button then re-dial

5 Replace handset Unused coins returned

SOS
Emergency calls
Dial 999
Insert no money

British **TELECOM** ®©

5D First on the right, second on the left

1 You are in the street near your home, *or* at the town centre in your home town. Answer these questions.

1. Excuse me. Where's the nearest bus stop, please?
2. Excuse me. Is there a car park near here?
3. Excuse me. Is there a swimming pool in the town?
4. Excuse me. I'm looking for the post office.
5. Excuse me. Where's the police station, please?

2 Put in a correct preposition (*at, in, on, from, for, under, of*).

1. 'Where are you ....?' 'San Francisco.'
2. She lives .... 37 Paradise Street.
3. Go straight on .... 600 yards.
4. I work .... the fifth floor.
5. Is there a fridge .... your kitchen?
6. I think your book is .... my coat.
7. 'Thank you very much.' 'Not .... all.'
8. Have you got a pen .... your bag?
9. 'Please sit down. Now, a few questions.' 'Yes, ... course.'
10. Tom's hat is .... the table.

3 Say these words with the correct stress.

bathroom   **car** park   living **room**   **phone** box
police   second   station   supermarket
swimming pool   TV   toilet   window

4 Add some words to each list.

1. armchair, chair, . . .
2. artist, doctor, . . .
3. bank, post office, . . .
4. bedroom, living room, . . .

5 Translate these into your language.

1. There are two bedrooms in the house.
2. There's a sofa in the living room.
3. My sister works in Edinburgh.
4. I live at 37 Valley Road.
5. My sister lives on the ground floor, and my brother lives in a small flat on the third floor.
6. Excuse me. Where's the nearest post office?
7. It's over there on the right.
8. 'Thank you very much.' 'Not at all.'
9. I'm sorry, I don't know.
10. Thank you anyway.
11. Go straight on for about three hundred metres.
12. First on the right, then second on the left.
13. How far is it?

6 If you have Student's Cassette A, find Unit 5, Lesson D, Exercise 3 (only the first set of directions is recorded here). Listen to the directions and try to write them down.

1   2

7 📼 Read this with a dictionary.

ITS A LONG STORY
4

Hello – is that Croxton 43122? Dr Wagner? Listen, Dr Wagner, this is Judy . . . Yes, Judy Parker. Listen, I'm in very bad trouble. Can you help? . . . Trouble with Sam and the bank and the police. I haven't got time to explain . . . Yes, OK. Please come to my house *at once* with your car. As fast as you can – it's really urgent . . . 23 Carlton Road. Turn right at the station and it's the second street on your left. *Please* hurry! Oh, and come to the *back* door.

Unit **6** **Habits**

6A What do you like?

1 Fill in the blanks.

1. '............... Mozart?' 'No, I ....'
2. 'I .... orange juice, but I .... apple juice at all.' 'Don't you?'
3. 'I like Picasso very much.' '............... you?' 'Yes, I ....'
4. What sort of books .... you ....?
5. Everybody .... Sally. Nobody .... Ann.
6. 'Do .... big dogs?' 'No, I ....'
7. Only two people in my family .... dancing.

2 Put in *he, she, him, her, it, they* or *them*.

1. 'Where are my pens?' '...............'re on the table.'
2. John's nice. I like .... a lot.
3. 'Have you got any dogs?' 'No, I don't like ....'
4. 'Is Mary at home?' 'Yes, ... is.' 'Can I speak to ...., please?' 'Yes, of course.'
5. 'Where are your books?' 'Ann's got ....'
6. Ann likes Bill, but he doesn't like .... much.
7. 'Are your children here?' 'Yes, ...'re in the garden.'
8. 'My brother's a shop assistant.' 'Where does .... work?'
9. 'Do you like shopping?' 'I hate ....'
10. 'Do you like cats?' 'No, I don't like .... at all.'
11. 'Is the car in the garage?' 'No, ...'s in the street.'
12. 'What do you think of Peter?' 'I quite like ....'

3 Say these sentences with the correct stress.

1. I like the **Greek** statue very **much**.
2. I **quite** like the **mask**.
3. The **mask** is **OK**.
4. I **don't** like the Vermeer picture **much**.
5. I **don't** like it at **all**.
6. I like the **Greek** statue **best**.
7. **Yes**, I **do**.
8. **No**, I **don't**.
9. I **love** it.
10. I **hate** them.
11. It de**pends**.

4 Read this and answer the question.

Four people work in an office: two women and two men. Anne likes Catherine, but she dislikes the two men. Peter doesn't like the person that Anne likes, but he likes Anne. Only one person likes Catherine. John likes two people. One person doesn't like Anne. Who is it?

(Solution on page 131.)

5 Write a poem about your likes and dislikes. Use a dictionary if you want to. Example:

I quite like the sea.
I like my friends and my family.
I love the sun, strawberries, dancing and cats.
I don't like fast cars or snails.
I hate violence.

"You don't like my mother, do you?"

26

6B Where are you at seven o'clock?

1 Answer the questions.

1. Where are you at six o'clock in the morning?
2. Where are you at eight o'clock in the morning?
3. Where are you at ten o'clock in the morning?
4. Where are you at ten to one in the afternoon?
5. Where are you at a quarter past seven in the evening?

2 Write down the times.

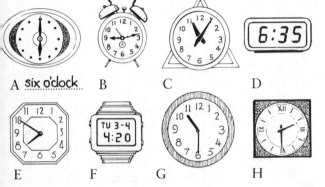

A six o'clock   B   C   D

E   F   G   H

3 Pronunciation. Draw the lines in box 2 to show which words rhyme with which letters.

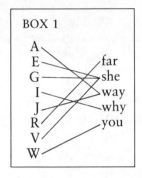

BOX 1
A
E
G
I
J
R
V
W

far
she
way
why
you

BOX 2
A
E
G
I
J
R
V
W

are
day
my
we
who

4 If you have Student's Cassette A, find Unit 6, Lesson B, Exercise 3. Listen to numbers 1 to 4 and write down the letters of the sentences you hear.

A. Thank you very much.
B. What time is your train?
C. Is that OK?
D. Oh yes, that's fine.

5 Try this crossword.

ACROSS

1. 'What time is it?'   'Eight ....'
5. 10 × 8.
8. This clue is number .... *across*.
11. At five o'clock in the morning I'm still .... bed.
12. Yes, ... course.
14. 'Do you like the music?' 'It's ....'
15. 'Do you like cats?' '................, I don't.'
16. It's under the first floor.
19. Half of two.
20. I live in a small .... on the third floor.
21. 3 × 2.
22. .... name's Michael.
23. .... is Judy. She is tall and fair.
25. 3.15 = a .... past three.
27. Is .... a table in the living room?
28. I like dogs, but I don't like ....
30. Half of 26.
34. 1.30 = half past ....
36. Good .... How are you?
37. Are you .... or single?

DOWN

1. The same as *12 across*.
2. I .... cats, but I don't .... dogs.
3. It's over there .... the left.

4. 'What time is it?'   'I'm sorry, I don't ....'
5. 'Do you speak ....?' 'Yes, a little.'
6. .... afternoon. How are you?
7. 5 × 2.
9. Judy is Sam's ....
10. 'Is your name Anne?' 'Yes, ...'s right.'
12. The same as *1 down*.
13. We live on the fourth ....
14. .... one person in the class likes maths.
17. .... you speak English?
18. The same as *12 down*.
21. 'Please .... down.' 'Thank you.'
22. I like music very ....
23. At a quarter to eight I am on my way .... work.
24. Are you married .... single?
26. Three threes.
29. Half of four.
31. She's a teacher. .... name's Alice.
32. My brother's .... engineer.
33. There are two chairs .... the bathroom.
35. 'Do you like dancing?' '................, I don't.'

(Solution on page 131.)

6C Work

1 Write *do* or *does* in each blank.

1. .... your father work in a garage?
2. What time .... you finish work in the evening?
3. What .... your husband do?
4. .... both your children go to the same school?
5. Where .... they have lunch?
6. .... your grandmother work?
7. When .... Andrew's sister have lunch?

2 Choose the correct verb for each blank.

1. Mechanics usually .... work at eight o'clock.
2. In Spain, people .... dinner at ten o'clock in the evening.
3. My cousin Tom .... in Germany.
4. The village shop .... at nine o'clock in the morning.
5. Anita .... children's clothes and shoes.
6. I .... cereal and milk for breakfast.
7. Brian .... old clocks.

VERBS	
have/has	repair/repairs
live/lives	sell/sells
open/opens	start/starts

3 Make eight sentences.

| Where
What time | do
does | Mr Carter
you
your sister
your mother
her children
Jane
Dr Wagner | work?
live?
have lunch?
start work? |
| | Do
Does | | work?
start work early?
work in a garage?
live in London?
have lunch? |

Example: Where does Jane have lunch ?

4 Say these words and sentences.

if it is six British English kitchen live listen
It is in the kitchen.
It isn't in the living room.

5 Read the texts. *Don't* use a dictionary. What jobs do you think the six people have? Possibilities: electrician, secretary, doctor, dentist, air hostess, photographer, bank manager, bus driver, artist, lorry driver, singer.

A. She speaks four languages. She works very long hours, but she does not work every day. She likes people and travel, and she travels a lot in her work.

Answer: She is an ...

B. She doesn't work in an office. She works very long hours, and she often gets up at night – it's a tiring job. She likes people. She does not speak any foreign languages. She loves her job.

Answer: ....

C. He gets up at half past seven every day, has breakfast at eight o'clock, and starts work at half past nine. He works in an office; he has two secretaries and two telephones. He does not work on Saturdays. He likes people and mathematics.

Answer: ....

D. He usually gets up at eleven o'clock, and has breakfast at lunchtime. He works at home. He works in the afternoons, but not every day. Sometimes he works very long hours; sometimes he does not work at all. He loves his job.

Answer: ....

E. She lives in a big city. She gets up at two o'clock in the afternoon, and has breakfast at three o'clock. She works from 9 p.m. until 2 a.m. She goes to and from work by taxi. She does not like her job much, and she does not like the people where she works.

Answer: ....

F. He gets up at two o'clock in the morning. He has breakfast and lunch in motorway restaurants. He works sitting down, and he travels a lot in his work. He likes his job.

Answer: ....

6D What newspaper do you read?

1 Choose the correct verb forms.

1. Stan *have/has* breakfast at half past seven.
2. Karen does not *have/has* breakfast.
3. How does Karen *go/goes* to work?
4. Stan *go/goes* to work by bus.
5. My father *work/works* in Cardiff.
6. He does not *like/likes* travelling.
7. He *get up / gets up* at six o'clock every day.
8. He does not *work/works* on Saturdays.
9. My parents *live/lives* in a big flat.
10. What does your father *do/does*?

2 *It, them, him* or *her*? Change the sentences. You can use your dictionary.

1. I like bananas.
   I like them.
2. I hate whisky.
3. Alice loves children.
4. Children love Alice.
5. I don't like rock music.
6. Can I speak to Bill, please?
7. Do you like your work?
8. She loves fast cars.
9. I don't like Mrs Harris very much.
10. I hate rain.
11. You can't speak to John. He isn't here.
12. Do you like big dogs?

3 Put in *never, sometimes, often, usually* or *always*. (Tell the truth!) You can use your dictionary.

1. I eat bananas.
2. I go to the cinema.
3. I drink coffee.
4. I speak French.
5. I work at home.
6. I get up before six o'clock.
7. I eat fish.
8. I go dancing.
9. I drink tea.
10. I read poetry.
11. I watch TV on Sundays.
12. I play tennis.

4 Translate these into your language.

1. I don't like cats, but my brother likes them very much.
2. 'Do you like dogs?'   'Yes, I do.' / 'No, I don't.'
3. It depends.
4. What time is it?
5. ten past three; half past three; a quarter to four; five to four
6. She's at home.
7. He's at school.
8. Stan gets up at seven o'clock.
9. After breakfast, he goes to work by bus.
10. What time does Karen get up?
11. What newspaper do you read?
12. What sort of music do you like?

5 If you have Student's Cassette A, find Unit 6, Lesson D, Exercise 2 (only the first sixteen questions are recorded here). Listen to the recording and write down five or more of the questions.

6 Imagine how one of these people spends his/her day, and write about it.

7 ☉☉ Read this with a dictionary.

IT'S A LONG STORY

5

Dr Wagner and Judy are on their way to the airport in Dr Wagner's car. There is another car behind them, with a pretty blue lamp on top. Dr Wagner accelerates, and the police car disappears.
'But what's the problem, Judy?' asks Dr Wagner.
'I can't explain,' says Judy. 'It's too complicated.'
'I know what it is,' says Dr Wagner. 'It's that Sam. I don't like him at all. He's a very dishonest young man.'

'Sam is my boyfriend,' says Judy, 'and I love him. He has sensitive eyes and beautiful hands.'
Dr Wagner does not answer.

Unit 7 Counting and measuring

7A How many calories?

1 Write the full forms.

aren't _are not_
haven't   we're
doesn't   you're
don't   they're
I'm

2 Put in *I, you, he, she, we, they, my, your, his, her, our* or *their*.

1. We live in London. .... address is 17 Fox Terrace, Hampstead.
2. 'Where does your sister work?' '................ works in Sheffield.'
3. Susie and Ingrid are German – .... are from Dortmund. .... father is a bank manager.
4. My mother lives with .... second husband in Edinburgh.
5. My wife and I are architects. .... work in an office in the centre of Cambridge.
6. 'There's Mr Parslow.' 'What's .... first name?' 'Sam.'

3 Answer *Yes, I do; No, I don't; Yes, I am* or *No, I'm not.*

1. Are you tall?
2. Do you like cats?
3. Are you married?
4. Are you American?
5. Do you speak French?
6. Do you work on Saturdays?
7. Are you a student?
8. Do you like your work?
9. Do you like children?

4 Give the third-person singular (*he/she/it*) forms of these verbs.

work _works_

like   watch   get   go   finish   have   sell
study

5 *Do* or *does*?

1. Where .... your parents live?
2. What time .... you start work?
3. .... your mother like cooking?
4. .... you like your job?
5. How .... you travel to work?
6. What sort of books .... Mary read?
7. What languages .... Mr Andrews speak?
8. What newspaper .... you read?

6 Look at the picture and complete the sentences.

1 2 3 4 5 6 7 8 9 10

1. The __sixth__ person is a tall, dark woman.
2. The .... person is a fair, slim man.
3. The .... person is a fair, slim woman.
4. The .... person is a dark, slim girl.
5. The .... person is a good-looking, dark man.
6. The .... person is an artist.
7. The .... person is a photographer.
8. The .... person is a doctor.
9. The .... person has got a hat.
10. The .... person has got a book.

7 Reading for information.

For dinner, you have:
prawns (112g)
two pork chops and a baked potato
fresh raspberries (226g)
How many calories?

Answer: ....

(Answer on page 131.)

Food	Portion	Calories	Fibre g
Plaice, fillets, fried in crumbs	6oz (170g) raw weight	435	1.0
Plums Victoria, dessert cooking, stewed without sugar, weighed with stones	2½oz (70g), average-sized fruit	15	1.5
Pork chop, grilled	6oz (170g)	40	3.5
leg, roast	7oz (220g) raw weight, fat cut off after grilling	315	0
Pork sausages, grilled	3oz (85g), lean only	155	0
	2oz (56g), large sausage, raw weight	135	0
	1oz (28g), 1 chipolata, raw weight	65	0
Porridge	1oz (28g) oatmeal or porridge oats made up with water	110	2.0
Potato baked	7oz (200g), eaten with skin	170	5.0
roast	2oz (56g)	90	1.0
instant, mashed	1oz (28g) dry weight	90	4.5
old, boiled and mashed	4oz (113g)	90	1.0
new	4oz (113g)	85	2.5
boiled		60	3.0
canned	4oz (113g) drained weight	60	0
Prawns, shelled	2oz (56g)	20	2.0
Prunes, dried with stones	1oz (28g), four to five prunes	85	8.5
stewed without sugar	4oz (113g) cooked weight	70	3.5
Puffed wheat	¾oz (21g), average breakfast bowl	150	0
Rabbit, stewed	6oz (170g), weighed on the bone	5	0.5
Radishes, raw	1oz (28g), salad serving	35	1.0
Raisins	½oz (14g), serving with cereal etc.	30	8.5
Raspberries raw	4oz (113g)	95	5.5
canned in syrup	4oz (113g), fruit and syrup	20	8.0
Redcurrants, stewed without sugar	4oz (113g)		

(from *The F-Plan Calorie and Fibre Chart* by Audrey Eyton)

7B It's terrible

1 Put in *the* where necessary.

1. 'There's a small piece of cheese and a small orange in the fridge.'   'I'll have .... cheese.'
2. .... rump steak is very expensive.
3. There are no calories in .... tea.
4. 'Where's .... milk?' 'In the fridge.'
5. .... boys and .... girls like imagining they're adults.
6. She's got two boys and two girls. .... girls are both fair, and .... boys are both dark.
7. I like .... oranges, but I don't like .... orange juice.
8. There are 50 calories in 5ml of .... sugar.

2 Put in *am, is, are, was, were*.

1. I .... an accountant – what do you do?
2. I .... in Patterson's yesterday.
3. Milk .... not so expensive when I .... a child.
4. Where in China .... Shanghai?
5. .... both your sisters in Britain?
6. My grandchildren .... here yesterday.
7. .... you tall as a child?
8. .... your son tall?

3 Give the prices of some things. Example:

Oranges are 75 cents a kilo.

4 Choose negative answers from the box.

1. 'Are you Spanish?'
2. 'Do you know what time it is?'
3. 'Is he married?'
4. 'Does Mary live with her parents?'
5. 'Are we in London?'
6. 'Am I speaking to Mrs Collins?'
7. 'Do they drink beer?'
8. 'Does he speak Chinese?'
9. 'Are they married?'

'No, I'm not.'	'No, I don't.'
'No, you aren't.'	'No, you don't.'
'No, he/she isn't.'	'No, he/she doesn't.'
'No, we aren't.'	'No, we don't.'
'No, they aren't.'	'No, they don't.'

5 If you have Student's Cassette A, find Unit 7, Lesson B, Exercise 1 (only the last part of the conversation is recorded here). Listen, and write down five or more sentences. Check with Student's Book Exercise 1.

6 Reading for information. Read the advertisements.

How much will it cost to buy all of these:
a girl's bicycle, a winter coat, 12lbs (pounds) of apples, two Alsatian puppies (baby dogs), a Renault 12TL, a violin and three ducks?

Total cost: ....

(Answer on page 131.)

7C Have you got a good memory?

1 Countable or uncountable? You can use your dictionary.

butter [u]   wool □   sheep □   beer □   rain □   bread □   banana □
£5 note [c]   tomato □   bank □   music □   wine □   money □

2 Match the words and the pictures. You can use your dictionary.

a chicken   a glass   a melon   a paper   a potato
some chicken   some glass   some melon   some paper   some potato

3 *Some* or *any*?

1. There is .... apple juice in the fridge.
2. Are there .... tomatoes in the kitchen?
3. I've got .... nice friends.
4. Alice hasn't got .... children.
5. Have you got .... American friends?
6. There isn't .... coffee in my cup.
7. There aren't .... flats in our street.
8. Has your father got .... brothers or sisters?
9. I know .... nice people in Canada.
10. We had .... rain this evening.

4 What food and drink is there in your fridge/kitchen/flat/house? Use *some* and *any*. Example:

There's some beer in my fridge, but there aren't any tomatoes.

5 Put in the correct form of the verb.

1. What languages __do__ you __speak__? (*speak*)
2. They __do not know__ my address. (*not know*)
3. Where .... your mother ....? (*live*)
4. What time .... you .... work? (*start*)
5. Lucy .... on Friday afternoons. (*not work*)
6. .... Cathy .... reading? (*like*)
7. .... they .... German in Switzerland? (*speak*)
8. I watch football, but I .... it. (*not play*)
9. Robert .... dancing and tennis. (*like*)
10. Alexandra .... the violin very well. (*play*)

6 If you have Student's Cassette A, find Unit 7, Lesson C, Exercise 4. Listen, and write down five or more questions.

7D Not enough money

1 Put in *How much* or *How many*.

1. .... brothers and sisters have you got?
2. '................. English do you speak?'   'Not much.'
3. .... people are there in your family?
4. .... calories are there in a pint of beer?
5. '................. money have you got on you?'
   'About £5.'
6. .... cheese is there in the fridge?
7. .... languages do you speak?
8. .... children have you got?

2 Make sentences.

I haven't got
I've got

enough   a lot of
too many   too much

money.   work.   free time.
friends.   clothes.   . . .

3 Pronounce these words with the correct stress.

tomato	orange	weekend
water	memory	newspaper
banana	travelling	interested
intelligent	depends	language
terrible	everybody	holiday
supermarket	breakfast	

4 Translate these into your language.

1. Do you know potatoes are eighty pence a kilo?
2. Everything's so expensive.
3. It's terrible.
4. There aren't any books on the table.
5. There isn't any snow in the garden.
6. 'Are there any fair people in your family?'   'Yes, there are.' / 'No, there aren't.'
7. I don't understand.
8. How many states are there in the USA?
9. There aren't many people here.
10. There isn't enough light in this room.
11. I've got too much work.

5 Read the postcard with a dictionary. Rewrite it, putting in capital letters and punctuation where necessary. Begin: *Dear Mary, . . .*

dear mary
well here we are at last our hotel is very nice we're on the 14th floor with a good view of the sea the room's small but it's clean and quiet the food's good and there's always enough sometimes there's too much there aren't many english people here but there's a nice couple from manchester in the next room
love carol and jim

6 Write a similar holiday postcard to a friend.

7 📼 Read this with a dictionary.

IT'S A LONG STORY
6

'Single to Rio de Janeiro, please,' says Judy.
  'First class or tourist?'
  'Oh, tourist, please.'
  Judy checks in and goes through passport control to the departure gate. On the plane, she finds a seat by the window. A young man comes and sits down by her. Judy looks at him. He is tall and dark, about 25, and very well dressed. Judy is not interested in him.
  He has dark brown eyes, a straight nose, a wide humorous mouth, and strong brown hands with long sensitive fingers. He is incredibly handsome. Judy looks out of the window.

Unit 8 Consolidation

8A Things to remember: Units 5, 6 and 7

1 Put in the right prepositions from the box.

at	by	from	in	near	next to	of	on	opposite	outside	to	until

Michael is an accountant in a language school. He lives ....1.... a small flat ....2.... the fourth floor of a building ....3.... a small street ....4.... Tokyo. The school is not very ....5.... his home; he goes ....6.... work ....7.... bus, and leaves home at eight o'clock to arrive ....8.... work at nine. He usually does some work in the bus ....9.... his way ....10.... work.

Michael's school is ....11.... a railway station. It is very big, and it has got a lot ....12.... students. Michael likes his office; it is ....13.... the reception desk, but it is big and quiet; there are some pretty trees ....14.... his window. He works ....15.... nine o'clock ....16.... a quarter to one, and then goes to lunch. Then he starts work again ....17.... two and stops ....18.... five. On his way back ....19.... work he buys some food, and has supper ....20.... home. He likes living ....21.... Japan; he doesn't go home to England ....22.... holiday, but visits pretty places ....23.... Japan.

It is Saturday morning now, and Michael is ....24.... home ....25.... bed. ....26.... Saturdays he gets up at ten o'clock, and then sits ....27.... the living room to have breakfast. ....28.... Saturday afternoons he plays tennis or goes swimming. ....29.... Saturday evenings he usually goes out.

2 Write some questions for these answers.

1. No, she doesn't. She lives in Paris.

   Does your mother live in London ?
2. No, there isn't, but there's some in the cupboard.
3. At seven o'clock.
4. No, I don't; I go by bus.
5. Yes, there are two.
6. At 23 Banbury Road.
7. Yes, I was.
8. It's over there by the police station.
9. About a hundred metres.
10. In a post office in Bradley Street.
11. Eight three two, four five four seven.
12. By car.
13. Science fiction.
14. No, but I'm interested in rock music.

3 Complete the sentences.

1. There .... apples in the cupboard.
2. .... there .... ice cream in the fridge?
3. How .... students .... there in your class?
4. .... my friends play tennis, but not many of them play badminton.
5. How .... milk have we got?
6. There are too .... chairs in here.
7. .... too .... coffee in this cup.
8. There ....n't .... cheese in the fridge, but there .... eggs.
9. There .... seven people, but only five books – that's not ....
10. Are there .... fair people in your family?

4 Look at the table and make sentences, using *never, sometimes, quite often, often, very often* or *always.* Examples:

Ann often goes to the theatre. She never goes to the cinema.

ACTIVITY	TIMES PER YEAR	
	Ann	Joe
goes to the theatre	50	0
goes to the cinema	0	60
watches TV	100	50
plays tennis	20	100
plays football	0	60
goes dancing	50	0
goes to work by bus	0	276
goes to work by taxi	130	0
goes to work by train	100	0
travels by air	3	2
works on Saturdays	0	46
works at night	230	0
falls in love	1	10

5 *Believe it or not.* Read this with a dictionary.

There are 6,700 museums in North America. 52% of Australians, 39% of British people, and 11% of French people say that they are 'very happy'. Your brain is 80% water. More than one third of Britain's Prime Ministers went to the same school – Eton College. The Wrigley's factory makes 1,360,000 kilometres of chewing gum every year. There are 150 million bicycles in the world. Americans use 300 litres of water per day per person. Elephants sleep for only two hours per day.

6 Do the crossword.

DOWN

1. This has got rooms in it.
2. There are 1,000 of these in a kilo.
3. Not 'yes'.
4. 'Do you and Alice like ice cream?' 'Yes, ……………… do.'
5. Five people – four people = one ………………
6. I ……………… TV in the evenings.
7. 'Who was at home?' '………………'
8. 'A ……………… of rump steak, please.'
11. 'Do you know Alec and Jim?' 'Of course I do. ……………… live very near me.'
13. Tomatoes are £2.50 a pound. That's very ………………
14. I have this in the morning.
15. There are a lot of these in a pound.
16. ……………… you like coffee?
17. Does your sister ……………… television very much?
22. You have this at about twelve o'clock.
23. The same as *39 down*.
24. This is in the bedroom.
26. A tomato, ……………… orange.
28. What's in this water? 
29. What time do you ……………… up?
30. My sister ……………… work at 4.30.
32. ……………… dear.
33. 'Is your sister fair?' 'Yes, she ………………'
34. boy → boys; man → ………………
36. What time ……………… it?
38. Jerome has breakfast ……………… half past twelve.
39. It's twenty-five ……………… eight.
41. Food costs so much! It's ………………
43. Do you ……………… big dogs?
44. 
45. I, you, he, she, ………………, we, you, they.
48. Like very, very, much.
50. John and his family live in a large flat on the fifth ………………
53. 
55. There's some of this under my hat.
56. My brother ……………… to tennis lessons every Saturday.
57. Thirteen – twelve = ………………
58. Miriam is ……………… her way to work.
60. The hat shop is next ……………… the post office.

ACROSS

2. I ……………… to school by bus.
3. What ……………… do you read?
6. There's a man outside the ………………!
9. How do you ……………… to work?
10. Is there a ……………… pool near your house?
12. Pounds, pence, dollars, pesetas, francs, yen, lire, and marks are ………………
14. Susan is over there ……………… the reception desk.
15. There are a hundred pence in this.
17. I + you, or I + she, or I + he, or I + they.
18. My, ………………, his, her, its, our, ………………, their.
19. I don't ……………… tennis.
20. Morning, afternoon, ………………, night.
21. What time do you ……………… lunch?
24. You read this.
25. 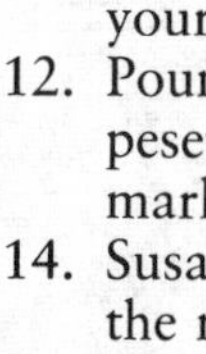
27. Hello.
31. I ……………… rock music; I don't like any of it at all.
34. she → her; he → him; I → ………………
35. 'Hi.' '………………'
37. 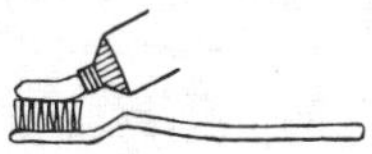
40. We ……………… work at nine o'clock.
42. A hundred – ninety-nine = ………………
43. I ……………… to classical music when I work.
46. You do this to books and newspapers.
47. A home, but not a house.
49. Half a litre ……………… milk.
51. Not small at all.
52. Don't like.
54. Where's my ……………… cream?
59. 'Where's the milk?' '………………'s on the table.'
61. It's terrible. Oh ………………
62. A sort of water.
63. There are a hundred of these in a pound.
64. A sort of street.

(Solution on page 131.)

8B What sort of house do you live in?

1 Put each verb into the correct form.

1. Where ....? (*you, live*)
2. How .... to work? (*Miriam and Stephen, travel*)
3. My sister .... in a large flat in London. (*live*)
4. .... in London? (*she, work*)
5. Everybody in my class .... Japanese. (*speak*)
6. My brother .... in Britain. (*not live*)
7. I .... some Spanish, but I .... much. (*speak; not understand*)
8. What sort of food ....? (*they, like*)
9. .... near their parents? (*Teresa and Patricio, live*)
10. '............ Shelagh Anderson?' 'No, I don't.' (*you, know*)
11. '............ a newspaper on Sundays?' 'Yes, ... *The Observer*.' (*you, read; I, read*)
12. What time .... to bed? (*your children, go*)
13. My sister and her husband haven't got a car; .... to work by bus. (*they, go*)
14. My sister and I .... shopping, but my brother .... it. (*dislike; love*)
15. '............ tennis?' 'No, but my sister .... very well.' (*your brother, play; play*)

2 Pronunciation. Say these sentences with the correct stress.

1. I **live** in **Cur**zon **Street**.
2. Do you **like coffee**?
3. **Yes**, I **do**.
4. **No**, I **don't**.
5. **What time** does **Karen get up**?
6. **Does** she **have break**fast?
7. **Yes**, she **does**.
8. **No**, she **doesn't**.
9. **Sam** and **Vir**ginia **live** in **Leeds**.

3 Spelling. Write the third person (*he/she/it*) forms.

cost _costs_

dislike get go hate like listen to
live love play read start stop travel
try watch work

4 If you have Student's Cassette A, find Unit 8, Lesson B, Exercise 3 (only the first part of the conversation is recorded here). Listen; mark a ✓ if you hear the same question, or write the question if it is different.

1. Is it a flat?
2. How many rooms has it got?
3. And your living room?
4. Do you play some sport?
5. Do you listen to classical music?

5 Nathalie lives in a small city in France. Look at the pictures and write what she does each evening. Example:

On Sundays she watches football or reads.

Su

Th

M

F

Tu

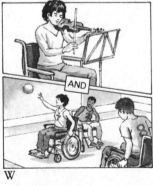
W Sa

6 Do you want an English-speaking pen friend? Then follow these steps:

1. Copy the form and fill it in clearly in CAPITAL letters.
2. Put your own address on an envelope. Don't put a stamp on the envelope.
3. Go to a main post office and buy FOUR International Reply-Paid Postage Coupons (or TWO if you are under 16). *If you do not send the coupons, you will not get an answer.*
4. Put the form, the envelope and the four coupons in another envelope and address it to
IFL Penfriend Co-ordinator
Naddesrudsvn. 45
N-1340 Bekkestua
Norway
5. Put the correct number of stamps on the envelope and post it.

Application form (please write in BLOCK LETTERS)

Personal Information

First name	Surname	Married/single	Age
....	....	....	....

Address in full (including your country)

....

....

....

Male/female	Occupation
....	....

Hobbies/interests	Languages
....	....
....	....
....	....
....	....

Pen friend information

Age	Male/female	Country of choice
....	....	....

Number of *International Reply Paid Coupons* enclosed: ....
Envelope addressed to yourself enclosed? Yes/~~No~~

(if no preference for country, please write 'Worldwide'.)

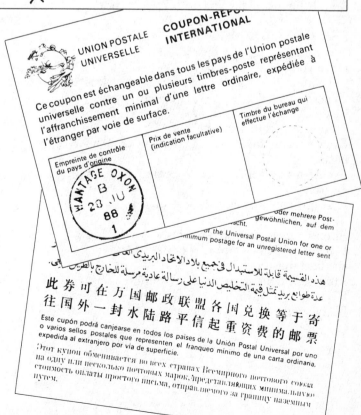

8C Choose

1 Pronounce these sentences with the right stress.

1. Are there any **fair people** in your **family**?
2. There are some **books** under your **chair**.
3. There **aren't** any **ap**ples in the **kitchen**.
4. Is there any **ice cream** in your **fridge**?
5. There's some **ice** in the **fridge**.
6. There **isn't** any **money** in the **cup**board.

2 Write sentences with *some, any, a lot of, too many, too much,* and *(not) enough.*

3. Put in *a/an, some, the* or − (= no article).

1. There's .... orange in my bag.
2. .... potatoes are very expensive now.
3. Is Joanna in .... bed?
4. I think John's on his way to .... school.
5. There's .... milk over here.
6. Does she go to work by .... car?
7. Do you like .... apple juice?
8. Have you got .... pen?
9. I live in .... small flat in .... Park Street.
10. 'Where's Jack?' 'In .... living room.'
11. I have .... lunch from 12.30 to 1.15.
12. John isn't here; I think he's at .... lunch.
13. Excuse me. Is there .... post office near here, please?
14. Excuse me. Where's .... nearest post office, please?
15. First on .... right, then second on .... left.
16. About .... hundred metres.
17. I've got .... interesting books about classical music.
18. Are you interested in .... politics?
19. How do you travel to .... work?
20. Barry's wife is .... engineer.

I LOVE YOU

38

4 Places. Where are these?

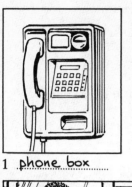

1 phone box   2   3   4   5

6   7   8   9

5
Look at the map on page 41 of your Student's Book and write directions to get to:

1. Lenthall Road
2. The Siger Road
3. Fairfield Place

6
If you have Student's Cassette A, find Unit 8, Lesson C, Speaking and Listening Exercise 3 (only numbers 1 and 3 are recorded here). Listen, and write down the directions.

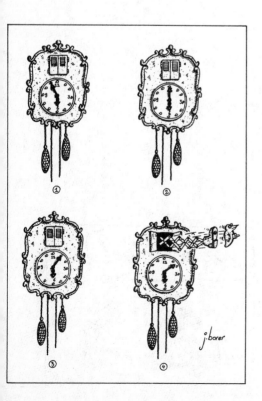

7 ▣▣ Read this with a dictionary.

IT'S A LONG STORY
7

'Excuse me. Would you like a drink?'
  'Oh, er, yes. Thank you very much. A whisky, please.'
  The young man gave[1] Judy her drink and smiled at her. He had[2] an incredibly attractive smile. He really looked very nice: calm, friendly and kind. 'Perhaps he's a doctor,' she thought[3] – 'a surgeon, with those strong sensitive hands. Or perhaps an artist, or a musician.' Yes, he looked like an artist. She looked at him again and smiled.
  'What time is it, please?' he asked.
  Judy looked at her watch. 'Two thirty-five.'
  'Thank you,' he said, and smiled at her. She smiled back at him. He smiled again. He took[4] a gun out of his pocket, stood[5] up, and walked to the front of the plane.

[1]gave: past of *give*   [4]took: past of *take*
[2]had: past of *have*   [5]stood: past of *stand*
[3]thought: past of *think*

THERE IS NO PRACTICE BOOK WORK FOR LESSON 8D.

Unit 9 Appearances

9A Sheila has got long dark hair

1 Make some sentences using *have got* (*'ve got*) or *has got* (*'s got*). Example:

A man in Philadelphia has got 26 names.

Mrs Calloway's flat   pretty eyes, Mary
You   a very good dentist
A man in Philadelphia   no word for 'snow'
We   four bedrooms in our house
Some Eskimo languages   three boyfriends
I   a big kitchen
My sister   26 names
My father   double nationality
Sam   TV in his bathroom
The President   enough money

2 Put in *and* if necessary.

1. Her hair is long ...*and*... dark.
2. She has got long ......—...... dark hair.
3. My boyfriend is tall .... intelligent.
4. John has got a nice .... good-looking girlfriend.
5. I live in a big .... old house.
6. Peter's eyes are small .... green.
7. My flat is small .... dark.
8. Alex has got big .... brown eyes.
9. Bill is a tall .... good-looking man.
10. Burford is a small .... pretty .... English town.

3 Put in *what, where, who* or *how*.

1. .... is your name?
2. .... is the station?
3. '............... is the woman with dark hair?' 'She's my sister.'
4. .... time is it, please?
5. '............... do you do?' 'I'm an artist.'
6. .... are you from?
7. '............... are you?' 'Fine, thanks.'
8. '............... are you?' 'My name's Colin Watson.'
9. .... old are your children?

4 Put in true 'short answers' to the questions.

1. Have you got blue eyes?
   Yes, I have. / No, I haven't.
2. Do you like classical music?
   Yes, I do. / No, I don't.
3. Have you got long hair?
4. Do you like coffee?
5. Are you hungry now?
6. Do you often travel by train?
7. Have you got pretty ears?
8. Is your home near a railway station?
9. Do you know any American people?
10. Has your teacher got brown eyes?

5 Practise saying these words. Be careful with the pronunciation of *-(e)s*.

-/z/	-/s/	-/ɪz/
doors	parents	glasses
names	nights	horses
plays	likes	buses
goes	stops	watches
potatoes	baths	oranges
Italians	works	noses
girls		houses
mornings		
lives		
eyes		

I JUST DISCOVERED WHY I'M SO CLUMSY. ...I'VE GOT 10 TOES.

..EVERYBODY HAS TEN TOES!

SEVEN ON ONE FOOT AND 3 ON THE OTHER?

6 Read these with a dictionary.

Jessica

My Mum

Jane is my
mummy

She is
nice is
my
mummy

May 12th
My mum is called Joy
and she is happy most of
the time as well and
she is very kind and she
looks a bit like me not much
Like me at all.

my mum.

Elaine

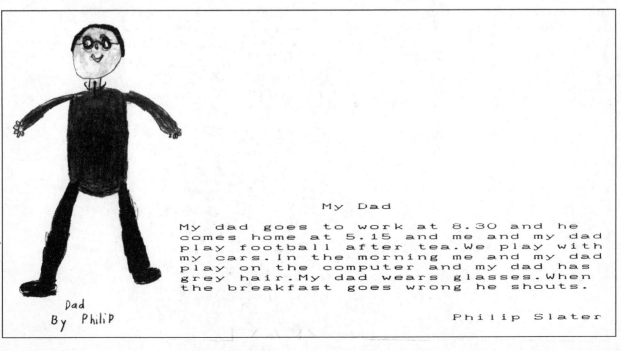

Dad
By Philip

My Dad

My dad goes to work at 8.30 and he
comes home at 5.15 and me and my dad
play football after tea. We play with
my cars. In the morning me and my dad
play on the computer and my dad has
grey hair. My dad wears glasses. When
the breakfast goes wrong he shouts.

Philip Slater

41

9B   A red sweater and blue jeans

1 What colour are these?

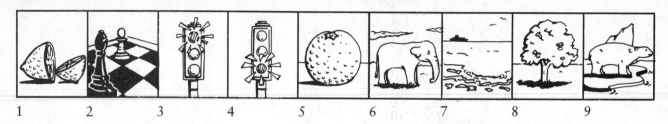

| 1 | 2 | 3 | 4 | 5 | 6 | 7 | 8 | 9 |

2 Cut out some pictures from magazines. Write the names and colours of the clothes.

3 Put in *am, are, is, have got* or *has got*.

1. I .... a small flat in London.
2. A Renault 4 .... a small car, but it .... four doors.
3. Where .... my trousers?
4. Her hair .... long and black and beautiful.
5. A spider .... eight legs.
6. Jane and Isaac .... four small children.
7. My father .... a big black dog.
8. There .... some beer in the fridge, I think.
9. Los Angeles .... in the United States.
10. .... there any people from Germany in the class?
11. Lucy .... two boyfriends. They .... called Sam and Alec, and they .... both very nice.
12. An elephant .... big ears and a long nose (called a *trunk*).

4 Put the words in the correct order.

1. blue have small a car we got
2. green yellow and I a dress am wearing
3. dark has long Jane hair got
4. ears have grey big got elephants
5. TV colour a and chairs green dark two are there living room my in
6. green ears , Sally long eyes has small hair and got

5 Complete the table.

SUBJECT	OBJECT	POSSESSIVE
....	me	my
you	you	....
he	him	....
....	her	her
we	us	....
....	them	their

6 If you have Student's Cassette A, find Unit 9, Lesson B, Exercise 4 (only the first seven questions are recorded here). Listen to the questions and try to write them down.

7 Read some of these advertisements with a dictionary. Which person would you most like to know? Which person would you least like to know? If you like, write an advertisement for yourself.

LATE IN LIFE, old but ......, needs companion for travel. Sense of humour essential. Box G58.

YOUNG MAN, lonely, wishes to meet warm, attractive woman, for friendship etc. Box G427.

EDINBURGH (m.) research worker, 25, not tall, shy, half Jew, half Arab, sincere, seeks interesting young lady. Box G382.

MAN, 23, Edinburgh, tall, intelligent, seeks female companion for genuine friendship. Enjoys theatre, music and travelling. Box G276.

MALE, 28, sks warm relationship slim, kind, gentle understanding woman, 30–50. Box G448.

FAT, FEMALE LECTURER, dyed hair, young fifties, once married, seeks humorous, tolerant, sincere man, for living-it-up. Arts, gardening, home-life. Box G30.

AFRICAN JOURNALIST, 35, 5'5", handsome and slim-built, seeks attractive London-based, warm, intellectual fun-loving prof female, 22–30, for lasting friendship. Will appreciate photos & phone number. Box G398.

TALL, GOOD-LOOKING DIVORCEE, forties, works in London, lives in country, interested in home life, walking, books and music, would like to meet unattached, caring, warm-natured man up to 60. Box G55.

ARTISTIC good-looking man, 28, wants soul-mate for lasting relationship. Please send phr......

female friend to enjoy life with. Ordinary, non-smoker. Box G84.

DAD, 30, widower; and baby seek female friend, wkends & holidays. N. Yorkshire. Box G732.

WOMAN, mid-sixties, seeks male companion, similar age. East Devon area. Box G512.

ATTRACTIVE, intelligent lady, mid-forties, seeks single, compassionate man, similar age, to talk, laugh with. Box G55.

UNATTACHED LADY, 45, not particularly attractive seeks ordinary man, 53/58, Surrey/Sussex, for happy relationship. Box G795.

SMALL, FRIENDLY, intelligent, red-headed designer, nearer 40 than 30, would like to meet man, over 28, black or white, warm-hearted, cheerful, hopefully non-smoking. Box G908.

ELEGANT, black divorcee, slim, 48, no children, wishes to meet tall, refined gentleman, 55–70, friendship/marriage. Midlands. Box G835.

TALL, SLIM, dark eyed Jewish widow, youthful, 49. Private Secretary. Sensitive, non-smoker, atheist, socialist, vegetarian, feminist, affectionate. Enjoys the arts, life, Woody Allen. Otherwise quite normal. Wish to meet male counterpart but who, unlike me, is solvent. Greater London. Box G31.

VIVACIOUS lady, mid-fifties, recently widowed, wishes to meet ......ing ....an for friendship.

9C   I look like my father

1 Write the contractions.

she is _she's_

he has got _he's got_

I have not got _I haven't got_

we are	John has got
you have got	John has not got
we have not got	they have
it is not	you are
John is	it is

2 Make questions with *have/has got*.

1. your mother | a car?
   Has your mother got a car?
2. she | a sister?
3. your parents | a nice house?
4. you | any coffee?
5. Mrs Hawkins | any children?
6. your house | a dining room?
7. you | a TV?

3 Make these sentences negative.

1. She's got blue eyes.
   She hasn't got blue eyes.
2. I've got some Italian friends.
   I haven't got any Italian friends.
3. We've got a garage.
   We haven't got a garage.
4. My parents have got a very nice house.
5. I've got some bread in my bag.
6. Peter and Ellen have got a Rolls-Royce.
7. Sally has got long hair.
8. Robert has got his father's nose.
9. I've got my mother's personality.

4 Make sentences with *looks like* and *does not look like*. Use *very, quite, a bit, (not) much* and *(not) at all*. Examples:

A camel looks very like a dromedary.
South America looks quite like Africa.
A cat looks a bit like a dog.
A radio does not look much like a TV.
The Taj Mahal does not look at all like a bird.

a modern train	Buckingham Palace	Africa
a camel	a dog	Stephenson's 'Rocket'
Chinese 你好嗎	an aeroplane / a box	a radio
India	the Taj Mahal	Japanese 日本語
a TV	a bird	a dromedary
a cat	a wolf	South America

5 If you have Student's Cassette A, find Unit 9, Lesson C, Exercise 3 (only the first two speakers are recorded here). Listen to the recording, and try to write down five or more words.

6 Write a description of yourself or a friend. Use some of these structures.

My name's . . . / My friend's name's . . .
I've got . . . / He/She's got . . .
I'm/He's/She's quite / very / not very / not at all . . .
I/He/She look(s) a bit / quite / very like . . .
I/He/She doesn't look (much / at all) like . . .
He/She and I are/have both . . .

"You've got beautiful eyes, Veronica."

43

9D Dear Mr Bell . . .

1 Make questions with *do you*.

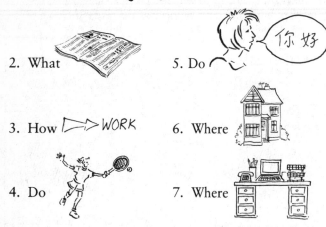

1. What time

   <u>What time do you get up ?</u>

2. What

3. How ▷ WORK

4. Do

5. Do 你好

6. Where

7. Where

2 Make questions for these answers. Use *does she*.

1. At seven o'clock.

   <u>What time does she get up ?</u>
2. *The Times.*
3. By car.
4. Yes, she does.
5. No, she doesn't.
6. In Scotland.
7. In a hospital.

3 Try to complete the conversation. Look at Student's Book Exercise 2 if you need help.

A: Mr ....?
B: ....
A: I'm .... journey?
B: ....
A: .... car ....
   Let's ....

4 Practise saying these words with the correct stress.

arrive   Tuesday   photograph   description
sincerely   conversation   station

5 Vocabulary revision. Do you know all these words? Can you pronounce them? Check in your dictionary if you're not sure.

hair; glasses; colour; face; eyes; sweater; trousers; letter; holiday; station; person; people; family; wear; read; dark; fair; grey; blue; black; small; pretty; slim; fat; tall; good-looking; left; right; who; sorry.

6 Translate these into your language.

1. I've got long dark hair, and my brother has, too.
2. My sister has got brown eyes and grey hair.
3. Pat is wearing a white sweater, a green blouse, and a green and black skirt.
4. I can't remember the colour of her eyes.
5. What are these called?
6. How do you pronounce this word?
7. Did you have a good journey?
8. Not bad, thanks.
9. My car's outside.
10. Yours sincerely,

7 If you have Student's Cassette A, find Unit 9, Lesson D, Exercise 2 (only the second conversation is recorded here). Say these sentences. Then listen to the recording and say them again.

Did you have a good journey?
Not bad, thanks.
Oh, I am sorry.
Paul Sanders?
Well, my car's outside.

8 Read this with a dictionary.

IT'S A LONG STORY
8

'Good afternoon. This is your hijacker speaking. We are now flying at 550 miles per hour at a height of 29,000 feet. In approximately one and a half hours we will be over the north of Scotland. I wish you a pleasant flight.'

Judy's head was going round and round. First Sam, then the police, and now the hijacker. Where would it all end? Life was really much too complicated. She drank her whisky. It didn't make any difference. She looked out of the window. The sky was full of big dark clouds. So was her head.

Some time later the plane started going down. The pilot's door opened, and the hijacker came out, still holding his gun. He walked up to her and smiled. 'You know,' he said, 'you really are extremely beautiful. Come and put on your parachute.' Judy fainted.

Unit 10 Wanting things

10A I'm hungry

1 Put in *am*, *are*, *is*, *has* or *have*.

1. We .... breakfast at nine o'clock on Sundays.
2. I .... toast and orange juice for breakfast, and my wife .... eggs and black coffee.
3. .... you hungry?
4. How old .... your daughter?
5. When I .... cold I like to .... a bath.
6. What colour .... your new car?
7. My sister .... got three children.
8. When my wife .... ill she doesn't go to the doctor; she goes to bed.

2 Make sentences with *when*.

1. John | ill | doctor
   When John is ill he goes to the doctor.
2. Mary | tired | bath
3. I | bored | shopping
4. Fred | hot | shower
5. Judy | unhappy | cinema
6. Sam | hungry | restaurant
7. Ann | bored | telephones friends
8. Lucy | happy | disco

3 Say these sentences with the correct stress.

1. I'm **very hungry**.
2. I'm a **bit tired**.
3. She's **not** at **all hun**gry.
4. **When Fred's bored** he **goes** to the cinema.
5. **When Lucy**'s un**happy** she **goes shop**ping.

4 Where would you find these things? Fill in the blanks.

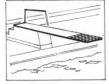
1. at a restaurant

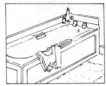
2. at a ....

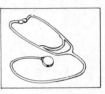
3. in a ....

4. at the ....'s

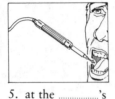
5. at the ....'s

6. at a ....

7. at ....

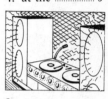
8. at a ....

5 Try the crossword.

ACROSS

1. Are you .... in English lessons?
4. When I'm dirty I have a ....
6. Not hot.
7. A .... assistant works in a ....
11. Not happy.
12. Have you .... any brothers or sisters?
13. When I'm .... I have a 4 *across*.
15. When you're .... you go to the doctor.
16. Excuse .... What time is it?
17. I'm .... I think I'll go to bed.
18. 'Would you like some bread and cheese?' 'No, thanks, I'm not at all ....'

DOWN

1. I go to work .... car.
2. 'Where's Ann?' 'I think she's in the living ....'
3. .... you have a good journey?
4. I don't go to work by ....
5. Not *11 across*.
8. The same as *5 down*.
9. I speak a little ....
10. 'Would you like something to drink?' 'No, thanks. I'm not ....'
14. A colour.
16. More than one man.

(Solution on page 131.)

10B Have you got anything in blue?

1 Put in the missing words.

A: Can I .... you?
B: I'm looking .... a blouse.
A: What ....?
B: 14.
A: Here's a lovely ....
B: Well, blue doesn't really suit ....
Have you got anything .... yellow?
A: Yes. Here's a nice .... in yellow.
B: Can I try .... on?
A: .... course.

*   *   *

B: How much .... it?
A: £19.95.
B: All right. I'll .... it.

2 Answer the questions. Use *a . . . one* with some of the words in the box (use a dictionary if necessary). Example:

'What colour car would you like?'   'A red one.'

large	small	modern	old	expensive
cheap	good-looking	nice	long	round
oval	red/black/brown/green	*etc*.		

1. What colour car would you like?
2. What sort of house would you like?
3. What colour shirt/blouse/tee-shirt are you wearing now?
4. What sort of watch have you got?
5. What sort of breakfast do you have on Sundays?
6. What sort of face have you got?
7. What sort of bedroom have you got?

3 Put in *he, him, she, her, it, they* or *them*.

1. .... looks like his father, and his children look like ....
2. 'What do you think of my new dress?'   'I'm afraid I don't like .... much.'
3. .... loves him, but he doesn't love ....
4. 'Here are two very nice blouses.'   'Can I try .... on?'
5. ....'s eight o'clock.
6. 'How are your parents?'   '...............'re very well, thanks.'   'Say hello to .... from me.'
7. John would like us to have dinner with .... next week.

4 Put in *a/an, the* or – (= no article).

1. .... languages are difficult to learn.
2. Ann is .... secretary, but she would like to study economics.
3. 'Where's .... car?'   'In .... car park in .... Cross Street.'
4. 'Who's that?'   'It's .... my boyfriend.'
5. Do you know, ... tomatoes cost £6 .... kilo.
6. My room is on .... sixth floor.

5 If you have Student's Cassette A, find Unit 10, Lesson B, Exercise 2 (only the third conversation is recorded here). Listen to the conversation and try to write it down. Then check with Student's Book Exercise 1.

10C Buying things

1 Practise saying these sentences with the correct stress.

1. **How much** are **those**?
2. There are some **books** under the **table**.
3. The **bicycle** is be**hind** the **door**.
4. The **table** is be**tween** the **win**dow and the **door**.
5. There is a **car** in **front** of the **house**.

2 Complete the sentences.

1. How much | those trousers?

   How much are those trousers?

2. Can | help | ?
3. Can | look | those shoes?
4. What | nice | shirt!
5. looking | French dictionary.
6. I'd like | try | on.
7. got | anything | blue?

3 Put in *at, in, of, on, to, until,* or *with*.

1. The train arrives .... Bristol Parkway Station .... 7.10.
2. 'How late do you work in the evenings?' '............... six o'clock.'
3. 'Where are Alice and Joe?'   '............... holiday in Scotland.'
4. Listen .... the recording.
5. Look .... the picture.
6. Your supper is .... the table.
7. 'Is the car .... the garage?'   'No, it's .... front .... the house.'
8. 'Are you interested .... politics?'   'Not very.'
9. I am quite short, ... dark hair and a small beard.
10. I always go to see my mother .... Sundays.

4 Put in *much* or *many*.

1. how .... people?
2. too .... water
3. not .... bread
4. how .... money?
5. too .... children
6. not .... time
7. how .... rooms?
8. too .... houses
9. not .... sweaters
10. how .... milk?

5 Look at the text, find the answers to the questions, and write them down. Time limit five minutes.

1. What street is the Hilton Hotel in?
2. How many cars can be parked in the Hilton garage?
3. How far is the Hilton from Victoria Station?
4. How many restaurants are there in the Hilton?
5. How much do guests at the Hilton pay for children if they sleep in the same room as their parents?

LONDON HILTON ON PARK LANE

ROOM 3181 Hilton International

Hotel Features:

- Address: 22 Park Lane, London W1A 2HH, England
- Telephone: 01-493-8000 Telex: 24873 Cable: HILTELS London
- Located in the heart of Mayfair, overlooking Hyde Park. Minutes from the elegant shopping and theatre districts
- 40 minutes from Heathrow Airport, 45 minutes from London–Gatwick Airport, 5 minutes from Victoria Station
- 446 comfortable guest rooms featuring:
  individual climate control
  direct-dial telephone
  electronic locks for maximum security
  radio and taped music
  self service mini-bar
  television with in-house films
- 54 one-, two- and three bedroom suites
- 2 restaurants, cocktail lounge and bar
- 24-hour room service
- Same day laundry/valet service at no extra charge (Monday–Saturday)
- Meeting facilities for up to 1000 persons
- 24-hour telex, cable, interpreter, secretarial service, typewriters, mail and postage facilities
- Pocket bleepers available for individual guest paging
- Worldwide courier service for documents guaranteeing one to three day delivery
- Teleplan – guarantees reasonable surcharges on international telephone calls
- Currency exchange at daily bank rates plus a modest handling charge of approximately 1% to cover only direct expenses
- Guest shops including beauty and barber, fashion, florist, drugstore, newsstand, speciality shops and transportation desk
- Indoor parking for 350 cars
- Hilton International Family Plan: there is no room charge for one or more children, up to the age of 16, when sharing the same room(s) with their parent(s) Maximum occupancy per room 3 persons

For reservations call your travel agent, any Hilton hotel or Hilton Reservation Service

10D Travelling

1 Complete the sentences with the expressions in the box. Use a dictionary if necessary.

how much	how many	too much
too many	not much	not many

1. We've got .... apples this year
   – we don't know where to put them all.
2. .... people were there at seven o'clock, but at ten o'clock the restaurant was full.
3. We can have dinner or just have a drink – .... time have you got?
4. There is .... snow in the mountains this year – not enough for good skiing.
5. I'd like to go on holiday, but I've got .... work.
6. .... people were at the meeting on Thursday?
7. There's .... bread – could you buy some?
8. It was difficult to see the Queen; there were .... people.
9. .... lessons do you have at school every day?
10. There were .... buses from my village to the city when I was a child.

2 Practise saying these words and sentences with the correct stress.

arrive   **break**fast   A**mer**ican   Ex**press**

1. **What** time is the **next** train?
2. I'd **like** a **room**, please.
3. **How much** is the **room**?
4. Can I **pay** by **credit card**?
5. Could you **speak** more **slowly**, please?

3 Vocabulary revision. Do you know all these words and expressions? Can you pronounce them? Check in your dictionary if you're not sure.

bread; friend; car park; dictionary; shoes; bath; shower; breakfast; money; night; number; room; speak; understand; arrive; next; under; outside.

4 Translate these into your language.

1. I'm hungry, and I'm quite tired.
2. The children are cold.
3. She's not at all thirsty.
4. When I'm bored I go to the cinema.
5. Can I help you?
6. I'm just looking.
7. I'm looking for a sweater.
8. Yellow doesn't suit me.
9. What size?
10. Can I try it on?
11. How much is that?
12. I'd like a room, please.
13. Could you speak more slowly, please?

5 If you have Student's Cassette A, find Unit 10, Lesson D, Exercise 2 (only the third conversation is recorded here). Listen to the conversation and try to write it down. Then check with Student's Book Exercise 1.

6 Complete one or both of these conversations. Look in the Student's Book if you need help.

A: time | train | York?
B: one | 4.45 | change | Birmingham
A: there | direct | one?
B: direct | 5.52 | arriving | 8.28
A: platform | 5.52?
B: 6

A: help?
B: room
A: ?
B: double
A: one?
B: nights
A: shower?
B: bath
   ?
A: £75
B: card?
A: form

7 Read this with a dictionary.

IT'S A LONG STORY
9

Judy opened her eyes. The sun was shining, and a cool wind was blowing on her face. She felt very light and happy. 'Where am I?' she said. Behind her, a man's voice said '100 feet above Loch Ness. Can you swim?' Judy fainted again.

When she opened her eyes, she was lying on the bank of the loch, with her head on her parachute. 'Allow me to introduce myself,' said the handsome young man. 'My name is Jasper MacDonald.' 'Why did you hijack the plane?' asked Judy. 'It's my birthday,' said Jasper. 'Now let's go to my castle and find some dry clothes.'

Unit 11 People's pasts

11A She never studied . . .

1 Write the past tenses.
Examples:

listen *listened*

hate *hated*

play *played*

study *studied*

arrive   change   help   live
look   love   marry
pronounce   remember   start
stay   try   watch   work

2 Look at Student's Book Unit 11, Lesson A, Exercise 1 again (and listen to the recording if you have Student's Cassette A). Write some sentences about your own past.

3 Express these times in another way. Example:

3.15 *a quarter past three*

9.20	5.15	7.40	11.55
9.25	3.35	5.30	7.05
10.45	6.10	1.50	

4 Pronunciation. Draw the lines in Box 2 to show which words rhyme with which letters.

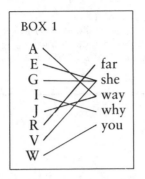

BOX 1
A
E
G
I
J
R
V
W
far
she
way
why
you

BOX 2
A
E
G
I
J
R
V
W
car
play
see
try
who

"I did say something, but that was yesterday."

11B When I was a small child . . .

1 Make questions beginning *When you were a child . . .*

1. happy?
   When you were a child, were you happy?
2. life | hard?
   When you were a child, was life hard?
3. sometimes hungry?
4. at home a lot?
5. your parents | happy?
6. your family | rich?
7. your house | big enough?
8. your father | out all day?
9. your grandmother | pretty?
10. your mother | very young?

2 Which word is different? Use a dictionary if necessary.

1. mother   father   friend   sister
   friend
2. chair   table   milk   fridge
3. hair   eye   moustache   beard
4. nose   ear   eye   hand
5. white   green   long   blue
6. shirt   trousers   shoes   jeans
7. small   pretty   long   mouth
8. bra   blouse   tie   skirt
9. hungry   restaurant   thirsty   tired
10. breakfast   restaurant   car park   swimming pool

3 Practise saying these words with the correct stress.

behind   between   different   enjoy   hotel
interesting   million   restaurant   thousand

4 If you have Student's Cassette A, find Unit 11, Lesson B, Exercise 2 (only the first speaker is recorded here). Close your book, play the recording, and write down as much as you can. Then open your book and check. Here is the text:

My name is Adrian Webber. My age is 42 years, and I was born in Delhi, India. This was due to the fact that my father had spent most of his adult life in India in the Indian police up to that time. I have a sister who's eight years older than myself. She was also born in India, and my childhood was very varied and quite happy as I remember.

5 Look at the three texts in Student's Book Exercise 1. Then write a new text using these notes.

- born small flat Berlin
- parents poor
- father shop assistant
- mother housewife
- sometimes hungry
- parents very good to me
- nearly always happy

11C   They didn't drink tea

1 How many years ago?

1. 1492

   About 500 years ago
2. 1970
3. the year when you were born
4. the year when your mother was born
5. the year when you started school
6. your tenth birthday

2 Make negative sentences.

1. She liked cheese. (*fish*)

   She did not like fish.
2. She lived in a small village. (*London*)
3. She played tennis. (*basketball*)
4. She studied maths. (*languages*)
5. She married a dentist. (*doctor*)
6. She worked in a university. (*office*)
7. She often travelled to America. (*Africa*)

3 Make questions for the sentences in Exercise 2. Example:

1. *What did she like?*

4 Write the text correctly with capital letters and punctuation. Begin: *Philip Hallow was . . .*

philip hallow was born in london in 1967 his father was a bus driver and his mother was a librarian they didnt have much money but philip and his two sisters jane and sarah were very happy children in 1984 philips father died so philip didnt go to university he started working in a bank but didnt like it so he changed to an import-export firm now hes the assistant manager and hes very happy

5 Say these sentences with the correct stress.

1. I was **born** in America.
2. My **father** was an engi**neer**.
3. My **mother** was a **teacher**.
4. We were **all** very **happy**.
5. I **liked** school, but I **didn't** study very **hard**.

"*My son? Good heavens, no – that's me a year ago!*"

11D Danced till half past one

1 What is the past of each verb?

marry *married*

want study have know come stop hate help
get tell shop

2 What is the infinitive of each verb?

heard *hear*

woke worked called died said could finished did
liked went

3 Write about Jake.

When Jake was 20 he was very poor, and life was difficult. He had to work very hard. But he had a good time. Now he's 40. He has plenty of money and a very good job. Life is easy. And he still has a good time!

THEN	NOW
Jake worked very hard.	*He doesn't work very hard.*
He lived in one small room.	He lives in a very big house.
He started work at 7.30.	
....	He works five hours a day.
He ate cheap food.	
....	He often goes to restaurants.
He did not travel much.	....
He played football on Saturday afternoons.	
....	He still has a lot of girlfriends.
....	He doesn't want to be an artist.
His mother worked in a shop.	....
....	He's got three cars.

4 Write a few sentences about what you did yesterday or last weekend.

5 Vocabulary revision. Do you know all these words and expressions? Can you pronounce them? Check in your dictionary if you're not sure.

age; friend; music; school; parents; teacher; question; window; travel; young; hungry; unhappy; tired; sometimes; never; quite; really; a bit; a lot; at home; except; between.

6 Translate these into your language.

1. When I was younger I hated school.
2. I changed schools five times.
3. I was born in a village in South Africa.
4. My parents were very poor.
5. My father was a farmer.
6. We were not very happy.
7. I got home at 3 a.m. again.
8. I couldn't find my key, so I climbed in through a window.

7 If you have Student's Cassette A, find Unit 11, Lesson D, Exercise 2. Listen to the conversation. You will hear these sentences, but there are some small differences. Can you find them? Check with Student's Book Exercise 2.

1. What time did you come back home last night, then, June?
2. About half past one, I think.
3. I didn't want to wake Mother up.
4. You know I hate loud music.
5. Why did you come home so late?
6. No, but we went to Alice's place and had some coffee.

8 Read this with a dictionary.

IT'S A LONG STORY
10

It didn't take long to get to Jasper's castle. It was an enormous building, about half a mile from Loch Ness, with tall towers, battlements and a moat, and at least 200 rooms. 'What a place!' said Judy. 'Well, it's not much, but it's home,' said Jasper. 'Let me show you to your room. And I'll see if I can find you some of my sister's clothes.'
  Judy's room was about ten minutes' walk from the main entrance, up a lot of stairs and along a lot of corridors. It was beautiful, decorated in light blue and lilac, with some wonderful pieces of antique furniture. There was a splendid view of the loch and the mountains. 'This is lovely!' said Judy. 'How many of you live here?' 'Just my sister and I,' said Jasper. 'And the ghost, of course. See you later.'

Unit 12 Consolidation

12A Things to remember: Units 9, 10 and 11

1 Look at the list of irregular verbs, and the rules for making regular past tenses, on page 56 of your Student's Book. Then read the story and write down the correct past tense verb form for each verb in *italics*.

I (*1. be*) very poor when I first (*2. live*) in Paris. When I (*3. go*) shopping for food, I always (*4. buy*) the cheapest things. I never (*5. travel*) by taxi; I usually (*6. walk*). But I (*7. be*) not unhappy. I (*8. love*) Paris, and people (*9. be*) very kind to me. I (*10. meet*) some people then who are still good friends today.

I only (*11. speak*) a little French, and I (*12. want*) to learn to speak and understand French well. Every day I (*13. get*) up early. Before my French lesson I (*14. read*) a newspaper and (*15. try*) to understand it; then I (*16. look*) up the difficult words in the dictionary and (*17. try*) to learn them. I (*18. go*) to lessons every day, and I (*19. talk*) to everybody I (*20. meet*).

After a few months I (*21. have got*) very little money, so I (*22. start*) a job as a part-time secretary for an American lawyer. The job (*23. not be*) interesting, but my life outside my job (*24. be*) very interesting. I (*25. have got*) friends who (*26. be*) artists, musicians and writers. I (*27. see*) and (*28. hear*) things that were new and interesting every day.

My family (*29. think*) I was coming home at the end of a year. Actually I stayed for five years, and I (*30. love*) every day of those five years. I (*31. come*) home in 1990, and I'm happy I did, but I think of Paris every day.

2 Write past tense questions for these answers.

1. She told me she was at home.

   What did she tell you? OR

   Where was she?
2. No, I didn't; I hated it.
3. I came by car.
4. I was quite happy.
5. No, but I liked rock music.
6. 6.30 a.m.
7. My mother was born in Ireland and my father was born in England.
8. We lived in Birmingham.

3 *Be, have, or have got?*

1. I .... not usually hungry in the morning, so I just .... a cup of coffee for breakfast.
2. My sister .... a very pretty cat.
3. How tall .... you?
4. That was a dirty job – I think I'll .... a shower before supper.
5. I don't know if they .... any children.
6. 'I .... cold!' 'Would you like my sweater?'
7. What colour .... your car?
8. There .... too many people in this room.
9. 'I .... very hungry.' 'I .... some bread and cheese. Would you like some?'
10. You .... beautiful eyes, Mark.
11. The children .... thirsty – have we got anything to drink in the car?
12. I think they .... artists. They look like artists.
13. I never .... lunch on Tuesdays – there's not enough time.
14. You .... your father's nose and mouth.
15. 'Would you like a cold drink?' 'Yes, please. I'............... hot.'

4 What are they saying?

1. .... English? / It's a compact disc player.
2. .... ? / I look a bit like my mother.
3. Can I help you? / ....
4. .... red? / I'll just see.
5. .... ? / £ ....
6. .... ? / It was terrible.

5

Imagine you are going to London by train to see Ms Hancock (an old friend of your mother's). Write a letter to Ms Hancock; say when you are arriving at Victoria Station, and say what you look like.

6

Find the answers to these questions in the text below. Don't read the complete text. (Note: *the Continent* means all of Europe except Britain and Ireland.)

1. I was late for the 12.10 to Cardiff from London.
   When is the next train to Cardiff?
2. If a standard-class ticket to Birmingham costs £5,
   how much does a first-class ticket cost?
3. Is it possible to buy a Britrail Pass in Bristol?
4. Is it possible to buy a Britrail Seapass in the USA?

TRAVELLING BY TRAIN

British Rail operates a service of 16,000 trains a day serving over 2,000 stations; there's hardly a part of Britain that can't be reached by train. A fast InterCity network links London with all major cities, such as Bristol, Cardiff, York and Edinburgh, with trains leaving the capital every hour during the main part of the day. Also, at no extra cost, you can travel up to 125 mph (200 kph) on the High Speed InterCity Trains to many major destinations.

On most trains you have the choice between First or Standard (Economy) Class. First Class seats are more spacious and cost 50% more than the Standard Class fare. Many InterCity trains have a full meals service, and grills, snacks and drinks are also available on other trains.

Buying your rail ticket

Overseas visitors are entitled to one of the best rail travel bargains anywhere – the Britrail Pass. It gives unlimited travel throughout Britain for 8, 15, 22 days or 1 month (7, 14, 21 days or 1 month in North America). Get one from Britrail Travel International Offices in North America or from local travel agents or major railway stations in Europe. Visitors from the Continent can also buy a Britrail Seapass. This covers all the facilities offered above, plus the return sea journey across the Channel. **Remember, these passes are not sold in Britain and must be bought before you leave your own country.**

Otherwise, in addition to the normal single return fares, certain tickets can be bought at reduced rates – see this page under heading "Lots of Travel Bargains". For general rail enquiries, go to your nearest British Rail Travel Centre or any railway station.

LOTS OF TRAVEL BARGAINS

How much you pay depends on where and when you want to

7 Do the crossword.

ACROSS

3. I've got four sisters, and we all look like our mother .... Ann; she looks like our father.
6. Were you .... when you were a child?
9. 'Are you ....?' 'Yes, I am; I didn't have any breakfast.'
10. Past tense of *come*.
11. I've got lots .... books about cats.
12. My brother looks very .... me.
13. I'm .... looking.
14. Not now.
15. Past of *hear*.
17. I .... some potatoes at Anderson's yesterday, and they were all bad.
18. *I see, you see, she* ....
19. You hear with this.
22. I'm looking .... some brown shoes.
24. You can have lunch here.
25. ...., you, her, him, it, us, them.
26. Where .... your sister born?

28. Can you .... me a newspaper when you're out?
29. One of the things you walk with.
30. 'We've only got two of these, a blue one and a red one. Which one would you like?' '................ red one, please.'
31.
33. What's your .... colour?
34. I .... up very late yesterday.
36. Have you got these in .... 7?
38. I was .... always happy when I was a small child.
39. The opposite of *live*.
40. Football, tennis, swimming.
43. Past tense of *meet*.
44. Infinitive of *went*.
46. I look a .... like my uncle.
48. Cheese is sometimes this colour.
50. Some people have got eyes this colour.
52. Who .... you look like?
53. I am .... wearing a jacket today.

54. Would you like tea .... coffee?
55. What a .... sweater!
56. Do .... shoes cost the same as these?
59. Are you English?
63. Six and four.
64. How do you .... e-i-g-h-t?
66. Not hot.
68. The opposite of *white*.
69. Can I .... it on?
72. There is a lot of this in England.
74. A teacher's is usually small; a rock star's can be very big.
76. I told my son I was at work, but .... I was at lunch with a friend.
77. Where .... you have lunch yesterday?
79. Is *go* a regular verb?
81. Did you .... your journey?

DOWN

1. 'Here's a .... of my brother.' 'What a good-looking man!'
2. I don't earn much, but my job is very ....
3. You see with this.
4. These things work with numbers.
5. The opposite of *different* is the ....
6. You do this with your ears.
7. .... sincerely
8. Not cold.
16. When I'm .... I have a shower.
20. Were you .... school on Friday?
21. The same as *72 across*.
23. The same as *33 across*.
25. 'When did you meet them?' 'I .... Alice in 1988, and I .... Joan in 1989.'
27. Can I give you .... to drink?
28. Think .... you speak.
32. Where .... you live?
35. Past tense of *take*.
37. The same as *81 across*.
40. Not tall.
41. She .... she was an actress, but actually she's a secretary.
42. A colour, but no colour.
45. Look! That's Susan .... there!
47. I'd like .... see something in green.

49. She's tall, ... blue eyes and dark hair.
50. Present tense of *went*.
51. *Love* is .... an irregular verb.
53. Eyes, ears, mouth, ...
55. The same as *53 down*.
57. Yours .... , Emma Stockton.
58. How was your .... ?

60. A thousand thousand.
61. Old people's hair is sometimes this colour.
62. Please come and see us .... when you are next in England.
65. Past tense of *can*.
67. Where is .... ?
70. This doesn't fit me very ....

71. A colour. Your favourite?
73. Not night.
75. .... I look round?
78. Have you got a pen .... your bag?
80. Is that your book .... the table?

(Solution on page 131.)

12B On Saturday

1 Add two or more words to each list.

1. chair, sofa, . . .
2. tomato, cheese, . . .
3. bank, post office, . . .
4. Italian, Chinese, . . .
5. I, she, . . .
6. under, in, . . .
7. hungry, cold, . . .

2 Put one of these words into each blank.

here	there
this	that
these	those
come/came	go/went

1. I .... here in 1975.
2. I go to .... hotel whenever I'm in Washington.
3. I think .... people over there are Greek.
4. I don't understand .... sentence. Could you come .... and help me with it?
5. .... grapes are very nice. Would you like some?
6. Could you pass me .... newspaper?
7. 'I love walking in the Himalayas.' 'Do you .... there often?'

3 Pronunciation. Underline the word that has a different vowel sound.

1. three   eat   people   ten
2. half   all   bath   start
3. watch   want   bank   what
4. some   come   love   home
5. cost   bored   course   tall
6. her   heard   first   ear
7. where   here   there   they're
8. time   night   live   child
9. sit   feet   in   if
10. would   look   who   foot

4 Make questions.

1. Des and Jo live in Santiago. (*Bob and Liz*)
   Where do Bob and Liz live ?
2. There are three rooms on the ground floor. (*the first floor*)
   How many rooms are there on the first floor ?
3. Ann has got two boys and a girl. (*Lucy*)
   How many children has Lucy got ?
4. There's a bus at three o'clock. (*four o'clock*)
   Is there a bus at four o'clock ?
5. My brother and his wife live in London. (*your sister and her husband*)
6. There's some cheese in the fridge. (*butter*)
7. I've got some English friends. (*American*)
8. My uncle Edward works in a bank. (*your aunt Helen*)
9. The 7.25 train arrives at 9.16. (*the 9.25 train*)
10. Celia and Jake have got three children. (*Fred and Catherine*)
11. There are two chairs in the hall. (*the kitchen*)
12. King Henry VIII had six wives. (*Henry VII*)

5 Who did what? Write sentences.

Indira Gandhi	made many famous films.
Van Gogh	wrote *Hamlet*.
Agatha Christie	was the first woman Prime
Shakespeare	Minister of India.
Karl Marx	discovered America in 1492.
Hitchcock	wrote detective stories.
Columbus	painted pictures.
	wrote *Das Kapital*.

6 Read these notes and then write a few sentences about Hemingway's life.

Ernest Hemingway b. Illinois 1899, d. Idaho 1961. Father doctor, mother musician and painter. Ambulance driver in Italy during First World War. Journalist in Paris after war for several years. Many well-known novels, including *The Sun Also Rises*, *Farewell to Arms*, *For Whom the Bell Tolls*, *The Old Man and the Sea*. Nobel Prize for literature 1954.

7 Write a few sentences about your life, or about the life of a famous man or woman.

12C Choose

1 Can you write the names of all the clothes?

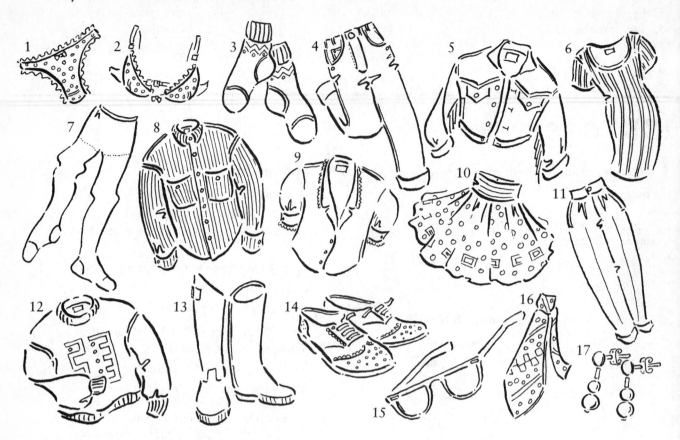

2 Circle the word that has a different stress.

1. **num**ber   **hap**py   (be**hind**)   **yel**low
2. station   hotel   thousand   village
3. income   arrive   depend   police
4. Saturday   favourite   interested   eleven
5. understand   afternoon   good-looking   engineer
6. British   Chinese   German   Russian
7. again   sometimes   toothpaste   breakfast

3 Write 'follow-up' questions.

1. 'Look at my new coat!'   ('Where | buy?')
   Where did you buy it ?
2. 'Mary's here.'   ('When | arrive?')
3. 'I'm tired.'   ('What time | get up?')
4. 'There were some French people at the party.'   ('How many . . . ?')
5. 'Karl Marx died in London.'   ('When | die?')
6. 'It's my birthday today.'   ('How old . . . ?')
7. 'I don't like pop music.'   ('What sort . . . ?')

4 Add -s if necessary.

1. I don't know where she work...S...
2. Does your brother live...–... at home?
3. He arrived........... at six o'clock.
4. My father hate........... rock and roll.
5. And he doesn't like........... jazz.
6. Do you know her........... children...........?
7. My brother........... are both very tall...........
8. Most people........... like........... music.
9. She's got........... beautiful long........... hair...........

5 Put in *some* or *any*.

1. I'd like .... milk, please.
2. We haven't got .... bread.
3. Is there .... cheese in the fridge?
4. I'm looking for .... cheap shoes.
5. Have you got .... American friends?
6. There aren't .... chairs in the room.
7. When I was a child, I had .... nice holidays in the mountains.
8. Did you do .... thing interesting at the weekend?

6 If you have Student's Cassette A, find Unit 12, Lesson C, Listening Exercise 1 (only the third conversation is recorded here). Find out what these mean: *scar; I've no idea*. Then listen to the conversation and try to write down everything.

7 Decide which sentences belong to the story about Queen Elizabeth I, and which sentences belong to the story about Princess Grace. Use a dictionary if you want. Write out the two stories.

1. Grace Kelly was born on the east coast of the United States in 1929.
2. Queen Elizabeth I was the daughter of Henry VIII and his second wife, Anne Boleyn.
3. When she was three months old she went to live at Hatfield, far from the King and Queen.
4. Her mother was executed by her father when the little girl was two and a half years old.
5. When she was 21, she went to Hollywood and began acting in films.
6. The young princess learnt Italian, French, Latin and Greek from royal tutors.
7. She appeared in the film *High Noon*, and won an Academy Award ('Oscar') for her acting in *A Country Girl*.
8. In 1956 she married Prince Rainier of Monaco.
9. She followed her half-brother Edward and her half-sister Mary to the throne.
10. She then retired from her career in America and devoted herself to her royal duties.
11. She never married, and ruled for 45 years as a strong and independent queen.
12. She was much loved by the people of England, and her reign was one of power and glory for her country.
13. She died in 1982 after a car accident.

8 🔊 Read this with a dictionary.

IT'S A LONG STORY
11

Judy had a bath, and then put on some of Jasper's sister's clothes. They fitted her perfectly. She looked at herself in the mirror, smiled, frowned, and went downstairs.

'Hello,' said Jasper. 'Did I tell you how beautiful you are?'

'Yes, you did,' said Judy.

'Fine,' said Jasper. 'Let me show you round the castle before tea.'

'But I don't want to stay for tea,' said Judy.

'This part of the castle was built in 1480,' said Jasper.

'I want to go to Rio,' said Judy.

'This is a portrait of my ancestor Donald MacDonald,' said Jasper.

'I want to see my boyfriend Sam,' said Judy.

'He was a friend of King James VI,' said Jasper.

'I love him,' said Judy.

'James VI?' said Jasper, interested.

'No, you fool,' said Judy. 'My boyfriend Sam.'

'Oh, Sam Watson,' said Jasper. 'You don't want to see him.'

'Yes, I do,' said Judy.

'No, you don't,' said Jasper. 'This is a portrait of my ancestor MacDonald MacDonald.'

'How do you know Sam?' said Judy.

'He was a friend of King Robert the Bruce,' said Jasper.

'Sam?' said Judy.

'No, you fool,' said Jasper. 'MacDonald. You don't want to see Sam. You want to stay here with me. I love you.'

Out of a door came an old man with white hair and very strange clothes. He was carrying his head under his arm. He looked very like the portrait.

'Who's that?' asked Judy.

'The ghost,' said Jasper.

'You don't want to go and see Sam,' said the ghost. 'You want to stay here with Jasper.'

THERE IS NO PRACTICE BOOK WORK FOR LESSON 12D.

Unit 13 Differences

13A I can sing, but I can't draw

1 Say these sentences with the correct stress.

1. Children **can't smile** when they're **born**.
2. **Most children** can **smile** when they're **six weeks old**.
3. **How many** languages can you **speak**?
4. Can any of you understand Portuguese?
5. We can **drive** you **home** if you like.
6. I **can't** understand where Jane is.
7. 'Can you **hear** me?' 'Of course I **can**!'
8. 'Could I **have** some coffee?' 'I'm afraid you **can't**; there isn't any.'

2 Write five sentences about things you can do (say how well), and five sentences about things you can't do. Examples:

I can sing very well.

I can swim a little.

I can't cook.

3 Vocabulary revision. How many words and/or expressions can you add to each list? Look at Student's Book Lessons 4A and 8A if you have difficulty.

1. dark, intelligent, . . .
2. mother, sister, . . .
3. China, India, . . .
4. Japanese, Swiss, . . .
5. engineer, shop assistant, . . .
6. never, sometimes, . . .
7. by, opposite, . . .
8. Monday, . . .
9. kitchen, bathroom, . . .
10. cooker, fridge, . . .
11. apple, bread, . . .
12. swimming pool, phone box, . . .
13. politics, music, . . .

4 If you have Student's Cassette B, find Unit 13, Lesson A, Exercise 2. Listen and repeat. Try for a very good pronunciation.

5 *Believe it or not.* Use a dictionary if you need it.

Gorillas can't swim.
Mice can sing.
Horses can sleep standing up.
Elephants can't jump, and they can't remember things very well, but they can stand on their heads.
A male emperor moth can smell a female eleven kilometres away.
Leopold Stokowski could play the violin and the piano when he was five.
Thomas Young (an 18th-century scientist) could speak twelve languages when he was eight.
The Danish linguist Rasmus Rask could speak 235 languages.
The American tennis player Roscoe Tanner could serve a ball at 225 kilometres an hour.

13B Better than all the others

1 In the following sentences, mark the stressed syllables like this: ⁓.

I can drive better than my brother.

Then mark the vowels pronounced /ə/: ○.

I can drive better than my brother.

1. My aunt can play tennis better than Steffi Graf.
2. I can ski better now than I could when I was younger.
3. I was good at football when I was younger.

2 Pronounce these words. If you have problems, look at Student's Book Exercise 3.

wake   cat   tall   map   past   saw   came

3 Make questions.

1. I run 5,000 metres every day. (*your sister?*)
   Does your sister run 5,000 metres
   every day?
2. I can cook quite well. (*your brother?*)
3. I can run 200 metres. (*swim?*)
4. My friend Susan came to see me on Saturday.
   (*by car?*)
5. My father was a dancer when he was younger.
   (*your mother?*)
6. My parents were very poor when they were
   young. (*unhappy?*)
7. George can type quite fast. (*How many words a
   minute?*)
8. We've got a big old piano. (*How many keys?*)

4 Read this.

Fish can swim better than pigeons can fly better than
squirrels can climb trees better than kangaroos can jump
higher than horses can run faster than canaries can sing
better than fish can swim . . .

Write a 'circle' about your family. Example:
I can run faster than my father can
cook better than my mother can ...

5 Read this, and try to answer the last question. You can use the table to help you.

'My four granddaughters are all very clever girls,' the bishop said. 'Each of them can play a different musical instrument and each can speak a different European language as well as – if not better than – a native of the country.' 'What instrument can Mary play?' asked someone.
   'The cello.'
   'Who can play the violin?'
   'D'you know,' said the bishop, 'I've temporarily forgotten. But I know it's the girl who can speak French.'

The rest of the facts which I found out were of a rather negative kind. I learned that the organist is not Valerie; that the girl who can speak German is not Lorna; and that Mary can speak no Italian. Anthea cannot play the violin; and she is not the girl who can speak Spanish. Valerie knows no French; Lorna cannot play the harp; and the organist cannot speak Italian.
   What can Valerie do?

(from *My Best Puzzles in Logic and Reasoning* by Hubert Phillips – adapted)

	cello	violin	organ	harp		French	German	Italian	Spanish
Mary	yes	no	no	no	Mary				
Valerie					Valerie				
Lorna					Lorna				
Anthea					Anthea				

(Solution on page 132.)

13C I'm much taller than my mother

1 Write the comparative and superlative of:

boring more boring most boring

pretty	red	thirsty	warm
cold	talkative	large	hot
young	cheerful	tall	long
rude	terrible		

2 Write the simple forms of these comparative and superlative adjectives.

slowest slow

funnier	oldest	cheaper	thinner
nicest	noisiest	bigger	smaller
worse	later		

3 Change the sentences as in the example.

1. I'm older than him. He's younger than me.
2. I'm taller than her. (Begin: *She's shorter . . .*)
3. She's bigger than me. (*I'm . . .*)
4. He's heavier than her. (*. . . lighter . . .*)
5. She's darker than me.
6. They're shorter than us.
7. Chinese is more difficult than Italian.

4 Make some true sentences. You can use your dictionary.

| The | highest mountain
smallest continent
largest ocean
largest sea
farthest spot from land
longest river
highest lake
largest active volcano | in the world is | Titicaca, in Peru.
the South China Sea.
in the South Pacific.
K2, not Everest.
the Nile or the Amazon.
Australia.
Mauna Loa, in Hawaii.
the Pacific. |

(Answers on page 132.)

5 *Believe it or not.* Read this with a dictionary.

Fair beards grow faster than dark beards.
The most common family name in the world is Chang: there are about 75,000,000 people called Chang in China. The most common first name in the world is Mohammed.
The oldest map was made 5,000 years ago: it shows the River Euphrates.
Rats can live longer without water than camels.
Nearly three times as many people live in Mexico City as in Norway.
One of the narrowest streets in the world is St John's Lane, in Rome: it is 49cm wide. But there is a street in Cornwall, England, that is even narrower: it is 48cm wide at its narrowest point.
Loud – louder – loudest: you can hear alligators calling a mile away. You can hear the clock bell 'Big Ben' (on the Houses of Parliament, London) ten miles away. When the volcano Krakatoa erupted in 1883, it was heard 3,000 miles away.
Cold – colder – coldest: There was ice on the river Nile in 829 AD and 1010 AD. On average, New York is colder than Reykjavik (Iceland). The coldest place in the world, in Antarctica, has an average temperature of –57.8°C.

13D The same or different?

1 Write six sentences about yourself, using *(not) as . . . as . . .* Examples:

I'm not as strong as a horse.

I'm as tall as my sister.

When I was two, I was as big as a

four-year-old.

2 Write sentences with *the same as* or *different from*.

1. your mother and your sister's mother

   My mother is the same as my sister's

   mother.
2. your nationality and your father's nationality
3. your nationality and your English teacher's nationality
4. your language and Italian
5. the colour of your eyes and the colour of your mother's eyes
6. your favourite TV programme and your father's favourite TV programme
7. your favourite music and your best friend's favourite music
8. where you live now and where you were born

3 Vocabulary revision. Do you know all these words and expressions? Can you pronounce them? Check in your dictionary if you're not sure.

language; afternoon; cat; pen; phone number; wife; woman; long; short; tall; big; small; nice; intelligent; good-looking; old; pretty; strong; cold; cheap; expensive; late; fine; far; interesting.

4 In English, most three-syllable words have got this stress pattern:

□□□
possible

In this list, there are three words with different stress patterns. Find the words and write them beside their stress patterns.

comfortable	good-looking	happier
anything	difficult	beautiful
expensive	understand	easiest
interesting		

Write the three different words.

1. □□□
2. □□□
3. □□□

60

5 Translate these into your language.

1. I can sing, but I can't draw.
2. I was good at maths when I was younger, but I'm not now.
3. I'm much taller than my mother.
4. Mario's a bit older than his brother.
5. A Volkswagen is not as quiet as a Rolls-Royce.
6. She's as good-looking as a film star.

6 Compare two people that you know very well. Write 100 words or more.

7 🔘 Read this with a dictionary.

IT'S A LONG STORY
12

Sam Watson was standing at the arrivals gate at Rio Airport, holding a bunch of flowers. He was worried. Judy's plane was three hours late and nobody knew why. Sam walked over to the bar and had a drink. He walked back to the arrivals gate. No news. He walked back to the bar and had another drink. Still no news . . . Back to the bar . . .

Two hours (and eight drinks) later, Judy's plane landed, and after another half hour the passengers started coming out. Sam smiled, and looked for Judy. After a time he stopped smiling. Finally, the last passenger came through. It wasn't Judy. Sam said a big bad word. What had happened? He went over to the information desk. 'My name's Sam Watson,' he said. 'Have you got any messages for me?' 'Yes,' said the stewardess. 'A telephone message from Scotland.' She handed him a paper. 'Mr Sam Watson, Rio Airport. Have a nice holiday. Don't come back. Love, Jasper MacDonald.' Sam said another big bad word, tore up the paper, and gave the flowers to the stewardess. 'What time's the next plane to London?'

Behind Sam, a tall beautiful girl was listening to his conversation. When she heard the word 'London', she smiled.

As the night plane took off, Sam closed his eyes. He loved travelling, but he was always a little afraid of flying. He couldn't really understand how the plane stayed up in the air. Also, he was worried about what would happen to him. Would there be detectives waiting for him at London Airport? It was crazy to leave Brazil. In Brazil there was sun, freedom and beautiful women. He could live happily for years with his £50,000. In Britain there was rain, trouble, policemen and a strong chance of prison. But he had to see Judy. Judy was different. Judy was special. Sam smiled and opened his eyes. Next to him there was sitting a tall, incredibly beautiful girl. 'Hello,' said Sam. 'My name's Sam.' 'I know,' said the beautiful girl. 'My name's Detective Sergeant Honeybone.' Sam closed his eyes again.

Unit 14 Personal information

14A How old are you?

1 Complete the dialogue.

DOCTOR: ...., Mr Rannoch?
PATIENT: 1 metre 76, doctor.
DOCTOR: Yes, I see. And ....?
PATIENT: About 80 kilos.
DOCTOR: Yes, right. ....?
PATIENT: 32.

2 Write sentences. Examples:

Beryl Jones is nineteen. She
is one metre sixty-two, and
weighs sixty-four kilos.

NAME	AGE	HEIGHT	WEIGHT
Beryl Jones	19	1m 62	64 kilos
Oscar Duke	37	1m 83	86 kilos
Tony Lands	14	1m 55	47 kilos
Amelia Berry	68	1m 60	45 kilos
Oliver Ashe	33	1m 75	104 kilos

3 Write the numbers in words.

135 *a hundred and thirty-five*
     OR: *one hundred and thirty-five.*

279	1,500	4,328	95,767
466	1,799	17,600	4,000,000

4 Write a description of somebody you know. How old is he/she? How tall? How much does she weigh? What does he/she look like?
OR: Describe your dream man/woman.

5 Write the times in words.

1 *ten to one*   2

3   4

5   6

7   8

9   10

6 Do the crossword.

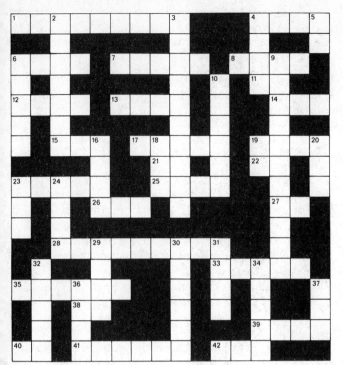

ACROSS

1. Not easy.
4. England is colder .... Brazil.
6. Spain is a .... country.
7. Past tense of *sleep*.
8. Your eyes are here.
11. She's on her way .... school.
12. A lot of water outside the house.
13. Past tense of *draw*.
14. Plural of *man*.
15. *Cold* is .... an irregular adjective.
17. Can you .... a bus?
19. Not bad.
21. 'Where's Yumiko?' '............... home – she's not very well today.'
22. Would you like coffee .... tea?
23. Can you .... in the daytime?
25. Take the .... right.
26. You hear with this.
27. I'm .... strong .... my sister, but she's faster than me.
28. On Friday, this is Thursday.
33. I am .... than my brother.
35. You can write with this.
38. 'Are you hungry?' 'Yes, I ....'
39. Can you make a ....?
40. My office is .... the reception desk.
41. Comparative of *easy*.
42. Infinitive of *saw*.

DOWN

2. In England, Spanish is a .... language.
3. You can use this to write a letter with.
4. She said .... she was at school.
5. Is *drive* a regular verb?
6. Superlative of *bad*.
9. My favourite chair is not very pretty, but it is very ....
10. The .... person in the world is over 110 years old.
16. I can't write very well, so I usually .... my letters.
18. Past tense of *run*.
19. Infinitive of *went*.
20. .... you see Mike yesterday?
23. My mother .... John Kennedy the day before he died.
24. Not difficult.
29. People do this in water.
30. A person who drives.
31. Is this .... pencil?
32. What's in your bag? It's very ....
34. Music helps you do this.
36. Past tense of *come*.
37. How many of these are irregular adjectives: *far, fast, fine, noisy*?

(Solution on page 132.)

METRIC CONVERSION HEADQUARTERS

PLEASE WIPE YOUR ~~FEET~~ CENTIMETRES

14B You look shy

1 Put in *look(s)*, *look(s) like*, or *like*.

1. Mrs Cowan .... a businesswoman, but actually she's a teacher.
2. You .... tired.
3. What is your new boyfriend ....?
4. I don't .... shy, but I am.
5. Alice .... her mother, but she isn't at all .... her in personality.
6. Japanese writing .... Chinese, but actually they're very different.
7. Why do you always .... so bad-tempered?
8. 'What's your job ....?' 'Boring.'

2 Put in *a/an, the* or – (= no article).

1. What's .... time?
2. My brother's .... architect.
3. I like .... steak, but I don't like .... eggs.
4. She lives in .... nice flat on .... fifth floor of .... old house.
5. Mary is .... John's sister.
6. What is .... your address?
7. What time is .... next train for Glasgow, please?
8. It's terrible – tomatoes are £5.50 .... kilo.
9. I'd like half .... litre of .... red wine.

3 Practise saying these words with the correct stress.

intelligent   personality   extremely
bad-tempered   talkative   optimistic   agree
information

4 Put in *as* or *than*.

1. I can sing better .... you.
2. Elizabeth's much taller .... her brother.
3. I'm nearly .... old .... my teacher.
4. Your eyes are the same colour .... mine.
5. Germany is bigger .... Switzerland.
6. Your problems are not .... important .... mine.
7. English is more difficult .... Spanish.
8. She likes the same music .... I do.

5 With a dictionary, read about your personality in the text. Is it true? Write a few sentences about yourself. Example:

It is true that I am energetic, but I do not think that I am bossy, and I do not agree that I am often bad-tempered. I look calm, but actually I am rather nervy. I think I look like a businessman...

Aries (21/3 – 20/4): energetic, bossy, often bad-tempered, warm, generous, sensitive, artistic.
Taurus (21/4 – 21/5): hardworking, calm, friendly. Interested in business, money, friends and family.
Gemini (22/5 – 21/6): clever, witty, very talkative, changeable. Interested in books, people and ideas.
Cancer (22/6 – 23/7): humorous, conservative, often happy, anxious, shy. Interested in history.
Leo (24/7 – 23/8): proud, bossy, independent; either very tidy or very untidy; passionate and generous.

Virgo (24/8 – 23/9): practical, punctual, critical, hardworking, perfectionist. Interested in nature.
Libra (24/9 – 23/10): friendly, energetic (but also lazy), pleasant, argumentative. Interested in sport, animals.
Scorpio (24/10 – 22/11): brave, sometimes violent, extremist, possessive, passionate. Often very religious.
Sagittarius (23/11 – 21/12): talkative, self-confident, cheerful. Interested in sport, travel, living dangerously.

Capricorn (22/12 – 20/1): conservative, polite, serious, sociable but shy. Interested in home, politics, people.
Aquarius (21/1 – 19/2): tolerant, sociable but unstable. Interested in sport and politics. Often brilliant or mad.
Pisces (20/2 – 20/3): sensitive, emotional, imaginative, artistic, depressive. Very interested in themselves.

It's not true! I'm not talkative! I'm not talkative! I'm not talkative! I'm n

6 Read this with a dictionary. Which is the picture of Leamas?

Leamas was a short man with close, iron-grey hair, and the physique of a swimmer. He was very strong. This strength was discernible in his back and shoulders, in his neck, and in the stubby formation of his hands and fingers.

He had a utilitarian approach to clothes, as he did to most other things, and even the spectacles he occasionally wore had steel rims. Most of his suits were of artificial fibre, none of them had waistcoats. He favoured shirts of the American kind with buttons on the points of the collars, and suede shoes with rubber soles.

He had an attractive face, muscular, and a stubborn line to his thin mouth. His eyes were brown and small; Irish, some said. He looked like a man who could make trouble, a man who looked after his money, a man who was not quite a gentleman.

The air hostess thought he was interesting. She guessed he was North Country, which he might have been, and rich, which he was not. She put his age at about fifty, which was about right. She guessed he was single, which was half true. Somewhere long ago there had been a divorce; somewhere there were children, now in their teens.

'If you want another whisky,' said the air hostess, 'you'd better hurry. We shall be at London Airport in twenty minutes.'

'No more.' He didn't look at her; he was looking out of the window at the grey-green fields of Kent.

(from *The Spy Who Came in From The Cold* by John Le Carré – adapted)

14C When is your birthday?

1 Say these dates.

21 June 1919
(*'June the twenty-first, nineteen nineteen'*)

8 May 1986	3 October 1844
17 July 1600	11 March 1011
12 December 1945	20 November 1907

2 Answer the questions. Use a dictionary.

1. What is the date today?
2. What day is it?
3. What is the time? (Answer in words, not figures.)
4. What day is tomorrow?
5. What day was yesterday?
6. What day is your birthday this year?
7. If today is 28 February 1992, what is tomorrow's date?
8. If today is Friday, what is the day after tomorrow? What was the day before yesterday?
9. If the day before yesterday was Friday, is the day after tomorrow Tuesday?
10. What is the day after the day before the day after the day before tomorrow?
11. What month comes before August?
12. What month comes after May?
13. Seven days = one ....
14. 365 days = one ....

3 Practise saying these words with the correct stress.

yesterday   today   tomorrow   July
September   April   **bir**thday

4 If you have Student's Cassette B, find Unit 14, Lesson C, Exercise 1. Practise saying the names of the months.

→

5 Read this description of picture A. Then complete the description of picture B.

This is a picture of a small dark room. There are only three pieces of furniture: a chair, a table and a cupboard. There are two people in the room – a man and a woman. The man is standing by the window talking to the woman, who is sitting at the table.

This is a picture of a .... There are fourteen ....: ...., ... and .... There are .... in the room – a woman .... The .... talking ...., who ....

A

B

6 Describe the room that you are in now.

7 *Believe it or not.* Read this with a dictionary.

Human fossils found in Tanzania are about 3,500,000 years old.

There is a tree in California that is 4,600 years old.

A sequoia tree in California is 272ft (83m) tall, and 79ft (24m) round. It contains enough wood to make 500,000,000 matches.

A cat in Devon lived to the age of 36.

On June 19, 1944, a dog in Pennsylvania had 23 puppies.

A blue whale can measure 110ft 2½in (33.58m) long, and weigh 187 tons.

Living bacteria dating from 1,500 years ago have been found in a Cumbrian lake.

The eye of a giant squid is 15 inches (38cm) across.

Cheetahs can run at up to 63 miles an hour (101km an hour).

The three-toed sloth (found in tropical America) travels at 8ft (2.44m) a minute when it is in a hurry.

(from the *Guinness Book of Records*)

14D Could I speak to Dan?

1 Write questions for the following answers. Begin *What sort of . . .* or *How many . . .*

1. Jazz.
2. Three – two boys and a girl.
3. 365.
4. Four and a kitchen.
5. Detective stories.
6. A big red one.
7. Thirteen.
8. Two and a half.

2 Put in suitable expressions.

ANN: Cambridge 342266.
BOB: Hi. .... is Bob. Is .... Ann?
ANN: Yes. Hi, Bob.
BOB: .... I speak to Jill?
ANN: I'm afraid she's not .... at the moment. Can I ....?
BOB: Yes, could you .... her to phone me when she gets home?
ANN: OK. I'll tell her.
BOB: Thanks a lot.
ANN: You're .... Bye.
BOB: ....

3 Singular countable noun, plural countable noun or uncountable noun? Make three lists with the words from the box. Can you put in any more words?

SINGULAR COUNTABLE	PLURAL COUNTABLE	UNCOUNTABLE
shirt	ears	hair

> shirt   eye   hair   ear-rings   ears
> jeans   glasses   water   watch   apple
> beer   snow   foot   bank   money   feet
> pounds   people   trousers   news

4 Vocabulary revision. Do you know all these words and expressions? Can you pronounce them? Check in your dictionary if you're not sure.

birthday; job; thousand; ask; different; heavy; nice; the same; both; other; o'clock; See you.

5 Translate these into your language.

1. The car is about 4 metres long.
2. I'm over 20 and under 30.
3. My mother's 66, but she looks older.
4. How tall are you?
5. 'What's today?'   'Tuesday.'
6. 'What's the date?'   'The seventeenth.'
7. the day after tomorrow; the day before yesterday
8. Is that Mary? This is Peter.
9. Could I speak to Ann?
10. Just a moment.
11. I'm afraid she's not in. Can I take a message?

6 If you have Student's Cassette B, find Unit 14, Lesson D, Exercise 2 (only the first conversation is recorded here). Listen to the conversation and practise saying the sentences.

7 Write about the life of somebody in your family. Example:

> My grandfather was born in 1940. His family lived ...

8 🔊 Read this with a dictionary.

IT'S A LONG STORY
13

When Judy woke up the next morning the sun was shining, the birds were singing, and everything was beautiful. Her room was lovely, and she felt fine. There was a knock on the door, and in walked the ghost, carrying a cup of tea. 'Did you sleep well?' he asked. 'Yes, beautifully,' said Judy. 'And thank you for a wonderful dinner last night.' The ghost blushed. 'Not at all,' he said. 'It was just a simple meal. I'm glad you enjoyed it.'

The evening before, after a magnificent dinner (cooked by the ghost), Judy and Jasper had talked far into the night – about life, love, art, death, music, books, travel, philosophy, religion, politics, economics, astronomy, biochemistry, archaeology, motor-racing and many other subjects. Most of all, they had talked about themselves. And when they had said goodnight, Jasper had kissed her, very gently. She could still feel the touch of his lips. What a perfect evening! Judy smiled at the memory. She stopped smiling. She had to go to Rio to see Sam. Sam was her boyfriend. She loved him. The sun went behind a cloud. The birds stopped singing. Judy started getting dressed as fast as she could.

67

Unit 15 Present and future

15A What's happening?

1 What are you wearing now?

2 Say what some of these people are probably doing now. Example:

My mother is probably shopping.

your mother   your father
your wife/husband/boyfriend/girlfriend
your boss   your teacher

your Prime Minister / President
one of your friends
your children

3 Say these sentences with the correct stress.

1. **What** are you **doing**?
2. **Where** are you **going**?
3. My **mother** is **probably shop**ping.

4. Some **people** are **dan**cing.
5. A **man** is **lying** on the **floor**.

4 Write some sentences about the picture. What is happening?
What are people doing?

"And this comment from your music teacher – 'I hope your boy enjoys
his holiday as much as I'm going to enjoy mine' . . ."

15B   The Universal Holiday Postcard Machine

1 Write the *-ing* forms.

speak _Speaking_

drive   get   go   lie   live   make   play
run   shop   smoke   start   stop   think
wear   work

2 Complete these conversations.

A: Hello. Cardiff 945 5928.
B: Hello, Jenny. .... is Owen. .... Mike, please?
A: I'm sorry, he can't come to the phone just now, Owen. He's ....ing.
B: OK. I'll ring back later.
A: I'll tell .... you called. Bye.
B: Bye.

*   *   *

A: What ....ing?
B: Chocolate. .... like some?
A: No, thanks. .... like chocolate.

3 Listen and look around you – in the room, in the house, in the street. What is happening? Write five or more sentences. Examples:

Somebody is singing.
My boyfriend is reading the paper.

4 Look at the pictures and complete the captions.

1. It is ....ing.   2. It is ....ing.

3. The .... is shining.

4. The weather is ....   5. The .... is fine.

5 What did you do yesterday or last weekend? Write about 100 words.

"'Marvellous weather, wish you were here, Regards. Sam.' When we get back to the U.K., Miss Marbon, remind me that this branch needs a Xerox."

15C Who's doing what when?

1 Complete the conversation.

PAT: Hello, Waterford 31868.
MARY: .... ?
PAT: This is Pat. Who's .... ?
MARY: Oh, hello, Pat. It's Mary. .... ?
PAT: No, I'm sorry. I'm not. My uncle's
          .... to dinner with us.
MARY: Well, are you .... on Thursday?
PAT: ....
MARY: .... ?
PAT: I'd love to. What time?
MARY: Let's meet at eight at ....
PAT: OK. ....
MARY: ....

2 What are you doing during the next few days?
Write three or more sentences.

3 Choose the right word and write the sentences.

1. My sister's much *taller/tallest* than me.
2. She's the *taller/tallest* person in our family.
3. My mother's 45, and my father's two years
   older/oldest than her.
4. English is *easier/easiest* than German.
5. China is the country with the *larger/largest*
   population.
6. *More/most* people speak Chinese than any other
   language.
7. I think my English is getting *better/best*.
8. But I'm afraid my pronunciation is getting *worse/
   worst*.
9. Anne is the *more/most* intelligent person I know
   – and the *nicer/nicest*.
10. You are *more/most* beautiful every day.

4 If you have Student's Cassette B, find Unit 15,
Lesson C, Exercise 1. Listen to the conversation. Try
to say some of the sentences; try to write some of
them down.

5 Here are two logic problems. Try one or both of
them. Use a dictionary. (Solutions on page 132.)

A

Arsenal, Manchester, Liverpool and Tottenham are four
football teams.
Each team is playing against one of the others on the next
three Saturdays – a different one each time.
On Saturday the 12th, Arsenal are playing against
Manchester.
Manchester are playing against Tottenham on the 19th.
Who is playing against who on the 26th?

B

Here are posters for next week's entertainments in the small
Fantasian town of South Lyne. Unfortunately, extremists have
painted out all foreign names (Fantasian surnames always
end in -*sk*). The four missing names are: James O'Connor,
Maurice Ducarme, Richard Haas and Antonio Carlotti.
– Haas isn't musical.
– O'Connor is leaving Fantasia on the morning of the 22nd.
– Ducarme is a famous actor.
Who is doing what when?

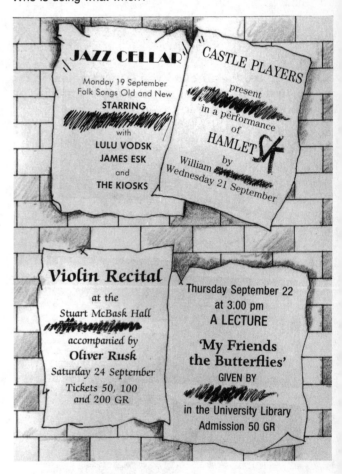

70

15D We're leaving on Monday

1 Put in the missing words.

1. 60 minutes = 1 ....
2. 24 .... = 1 ....
3. 7 .... = 1 ....
4. 28 or 29 or 30 or 31
   .... = 1 ....
5. 12 .... = 1 ....

2 Answer the questions.

1. How soon is your birthday? In a few weeks? In three months?
2. How soon is Christmas?
3. How soon is your next English lesson?
4. How soon is the year 2000?
5. How soon is next Tuesday?
6. How soon is your next holiday?

3 Put in *at, on, in, for* or no preposition.

1. Are you free .... Friday evening?
2. Can you come round to my place .... nine o'clock tomorrow?
3. It's my birthday .... three days.
4. 'We're going to California.' 'How long ....?' 'Three weeks.'
5. We haven't got time to go shopping – the shops close .... five minutes.
6. What are you doing .... next Tuesday?
7. Can I talk to you .... five minutes?

4 Imagine that you are going on a journey round the world, starting next Monday. Write about your schedule. Useful words: *fly, stay, drive, hire.* Example:

On Monday I'm flying to New York. I'm staying in New York for three or four days; then I'm hiring a car and driving to Los Angeles. Then . . .

5 Vocabulary revision. Do you know all these words and expressions? Can you pronounce them? Check in your dictionary if you're not sure.

weekend; dance; get up; work; play; watch; drive; eat; sing; sleep; smoke; stand; read; write; make; happen; beautiful; really; probably; anything; this evening; Would you like to . . . ?

6 Translate these into your language.

1. What's happening?
2. What are you doing?
3. My mother is probably shopping just now.
4. The sun is shining.
5. We are having a good time.
6. Tomorrow we are going to London.
7. Are you doing anything this evening?
8. 'Would you like to see a film with me?' 'I'm sorry, I'm not free.'
9. She's the most intelligent person I know.
10. 'I'm going to America in April.' 'That's nice. How long for?'

7 ⊙⊙ Read this with a dictionary.

IT'S A LONG STORY
14

When Sam woke up he felt terrible. He had a headache, and there was a horrible taste in his mouth. He looked out of the window. The sun was shining, and through a gap in the clouds he could see the sea. It was a long way down. Sam shivered and turned to look at Detective Sergeant Honeybone. She looked fresh and lovely – even more beautiful than the evening before. 'Good morning,' she said. 'Did you sleep well?' 'No,' said Sam. 'Excuse me.' He got up and walked forward to the toilets.

After a wash and a shave, Sam felt a little better. He brushed his hair, put his jacket back on, and looked at his tongue in the mirror. Not a pretty sight. Sam put his tongue back in, took out his gun, and looked at his watch. Time to move. He came out of the toilet, glanced round quickly, and then walked to the front of the plane. Opening the door of the cockpit, he stepped inside. 'This is a hijack,' he said. 'Take me to Loch Ness.' 'Oh God,' said the pilot. 'Not again. What's so special about Loch Ness?' 'Jasper MacDonald,' said Sam.

Unit 16 Consolidation

16A Things to remember: Units 13, 14 and 15

1 Write the comparative and superlative of these adjectives. Example:

big *bigger* *biggest*

comfortable   economical
funny   heavy   high   late
long   noisy   quiet   slim
warm

2 Complete the sentences.

1. My boyfriend | same age | me.
2. He | much taller | me.
3. Who | best footballer | world?
4. I | speak English | a bit better | my father.
5. I think | I | as good-looking | film star.
6. England | very different | United States.
7. you think | you | stronger | me?

3 Write these dates in words.

17.10.88	18.4.1900
5.3.69	21.1.94
1.12.97	2.3.36
3.6.99	20.5.1908

4 Somebody (Alex) wants you to go out. You don't want to go out. Complete Alex's sentences and write your side of the conversation.

ALEX: you | doing anything | this evening?
YOU: ....
ALEX: Well, ... about tomorrow?
YOU: ....
ALEX: free | Thursday?
YOU: ....
ALEX: Friday?
YOU: ....
ALEX: weekend?
YOU: ....
ALEX: ....

5 Put in the correct verb forms and the missing words.

Hello, Mary. Yes, I'm sorry. I know, I (*want*) to phone you yesterday, but I (*not have*) time. It's crazy here. We (*leave*) the day .... tomorrow, and there's too much to do. Yes, China. We (*go*) .... six weeks. Jim (*work*) with some engineers on a big housing development in Beijing, and I (*give*) six concerts. Excuse me a minute – the children are very quiet, and I don't like it when I don't know what they (*do*).

*   *   *

Sorry about that, Mary. I'm back. It's OK. Sally (*watch*) TV and Peter (*make*) a cake. Yes, I know. He's a terrible cook, but if that's what he wants to do. No, they (*not come*) with us – they're staying with Granny .... three weeks, and then Sally (*go*) to Louise for the rest of the time, and Peter (*stay*) with his friends in Durham. .... about you? What (*happen*) with you and John? Really? So he (*change*) his job to be near you? I say, Mary! Perhaps this is the real thing after all these years.

Oh, dear, Sally (*ask*) for .... to eat again. Look, I can't (*talk*) any more now, but let's meet when we're back. Middle of August, OK? Thanks for phoning. Bye, Mary.

"But you're far too young to marry – why, you're only just old enough to go off and live with someone."

6 **Do the crossword.**

(Solution on page 132.)

1. If you go to this, you can see people playing football. (*Two words*)
8. When I was at school, I was good .... maths and running.
10. Mon, Tue, Wed, Thur, Fri, ..., Sun.
11. Can you .... all the questions?
13. Yes or ....?
14. 600 minutes = ... hours.
16. What sort of food .... your children like?
17. One and the other.
19. What time .... the next train leave?
20. Mike likes eating, but .... can't cook.
21. Would you like tea .... coffee?
22. A lot .... people can speak two languages.
24. I can't hear with my left ....
25. From another country.
27. I'm taller than her, but she's stronger than ....
28. The .... is shining.
29. Jan, ..., Mar.
30. Apr.
31. A lot of water between countries.
34. Can you help me? I don't know where .... glasses are.
36. A person who talks a lot is ....
39. 'What sort of discs do you want?' '............... doesn't matter.'

40. I don't think I'm free on Thursday – I'm .... going to a concert.
43. Your son's son's father is your ....
45. Five hundred years ago, people in Europe didn't drink ....
46. Are .... doing anything this evening?
48. Just the same as *27 across*.
49. If today is Saturday, the day after .... is Monday.
50. 'Thanks a lot.' 'You're ....'

DOWN ▽

1. He's stronger than me, but he can't run as .... as me.
2. Oct.
3. I think she's the most .... woman in the world.
4. What time did you get home .... night?
5. Present of *met*.
6. Could I speak .... Susan?
7. .... is not the same as *pretty*.
9. I've got .... much work to do.
12. .... is my favourite colour.
15. *House* is not a verb or an adjective, but a ....
18. Past of *draw*.
20. We weren't rich, but we were ....
21. Like *21 across*.
23. The month after the month before *29 across*.
26. Are you doing anything .... Saturday night?
28. Present of *sat*.
30. Sorry – .... I late?
31. I love the mountains, but I can't ....
32. A good thing to do with food.
33. Were you good .... maths when you were at school?
36. 'To be or not ...., that is the question.' (Shakespeare) (*Two words*)
37. Tomorrow we are going to Manchester. .... it will be wonderful. (*Two words*)
38. You can sleep here when you are on a journey.
41. See you .... eight o'clock .... the cinema.
42. Why did you come home so .... last night?
44. There is usually some of this in a newspaper.
46. 'I can run faster than ....' 'No, ... can't.'
47. I can't sing .... draw.
48. Excuse ....

16B Present tenses

1 **Put in the correct tense.**

1. I would like to go home now. It .... late. (*is getting / gets*)
2. 'What ....?' 'Beer. Can I get you some?' (*are you drinking / do you drink*)
3. 'Where's Lucy?' 'She .... a bath.' (*'s having / has*)
4. What sort of films ....? (*are you liking / do you like*)
5. 'Do you speak Chinese?' 'No, ...' (*I'm not / I don't*)
6. What time .... to bed? (*are you usually going / do you usually go*)
7. 'Is there anything to eat?' 'I .... some fish.' (*'m just cooking / just cook*)
8. 'What are you doing?' 'I .... the guitar.' (*'m just practising / just practise*)
9. .... tomorrow? (*Are you working / Do you work*)
10. No, I .... on Saturdays. (*'m not working / don't work*)

73

2 Pronunciation. Practise saying these with the correct stress.

1. **What** are you **doing**?
2. **What's** she **eating**?
3. **Where** are they **going**?
4. **What** did she **say**?
5. **How** do you **know**?
6. **When** do you **want** to **come**?
7. **What** **time** are you **going** to **work** tomorrow?
8. **Who** did you **see** yesterday?
9. **What** are you **doing** this evening?

3 Vocabulary. Look around the room where you are working. Can you write the English words for ten or more things that you can see?

4 Put the parts of the story in order.

1. 'Didn't I tell you
2. 'Take it to the zoo,'
3. said the man,
4. a man was walking in the park
5. 'I did,'
6. He still had the penguin.
7. 'and he liked it very much.
8. answered the policeman.
9. and asked what to do.
10. he asked.
11. Now I'm taking him to the cinema.'
12. the policeman saw the man again.
13. when he met a penguin.
14. Next day
15. to take that penguin to the zoo?'
16. So he took it to a policeman
17. One day

5 What did you do yesterday? (Write about 100 words.)

6 Read one of the texts with a dictionary.

A long wait
The female emperor penguin lays only one egg each year. She gives it to the male, who puts it on his feet and covers it with a special pouch. The female then goes to the sea, perhaps many kilometres from the male, and does not return for three months. The male stands in the cold, with no food. When the egg hatches, the female comes back and her thin, weak mate goes off to feed.

The robin
The robin is a plump brown bird 5½ inches (14cm) long. It has a red face and breast and a white belly. Males and females look alike, but the amount of red on the breast varies in individual birds.
   Robins live all over Great Britain and Ireland, and are often found in gardens. Each male or pair has a territory which the male defends.
   Robins eat fruit, worms and insects. The female lays four to six eggs in a nest made of moss and hair. The eggs are white with light red spots.

Brown

Red

White

Facts about gorillas
1. A big male gorilla can weigh 200 kilograms.
2. Gorillas build a nest to sleep in each night.
3. A big gorilla's hands are 2.65 metres from its shoulders.
4. Gorillas live in groups and only move about one third of a mile a day.
5. Gorillas are afraid of snakes.
6. Gorillas never have fleas.

16C Choose

1 Look at the examples and then put the words in the right order.

```
 1        2          3
Is your brother working today?
          1      2        3
What are those people drinking?
      1        2      3
Does Mr Allison play the piano?
         1       2        3
Where do your parents live?
```

1. does Wagner work where Mrs ?
2. fast does George like cars ?
3. eating girl that what is ?
4. often boss how on holiday does your go ?
5. this are evening doing you what ?
6. Smith dinner to us are Mr coming with Mrs and ?
7. for does what wife breakfast have your usually ?
8. Dr working today is Harris ?

2 Look at the list of words. Find something that is:

1. younger than the world
2. older than a house
3. heavier than a typewriter
4. funnier than a politician
5. more difficult than an English exercise
6. faster than a cat
7. easier than an English exercise
8. more beautiful than a car
9. more interesting than an English exercise
10. shorter than a year

Make some more comparisons. Try to make some unusual ones. Examples:

The sea is older than cities.
Love is more expensive than food.

a car	life	a teacher	love
work	a cat	food	a pencil
a typewriter	a boss	a week	
a month	a year	a head	
a city	the sun	the sea	
a mountain	a politician		
a child			

3 Practise saying these words with the correct stress.

interesting   **com**fortable
handsome   **prob**ably
welcome   **birth**day   ex**tre**mely
to**mor**row   with**out**   per**haps**
Sep**tem**ber

4 Put in *look(s)*, *look(s) like*, or *like(s)*.

1. She .... her mother, except that her nose is much longer.
2. You .... tired – can I help you?
3. What is your boss ....?
4. He .... more .... a businessman than a teacher.
5. Your voice is .... music to my ears.
6. 'Who does the baby ....?' 'Well, she's got her father's eyes.'
7. Mary always .... worried these days.

5 Use five or more of these words and expressions to write some true sentences about yourself.

didn't	woke	knew	came
went	lived	drank	started
stopped	yesterday		
last night	a long time ago		

6 Translate these into your language.

1. You look happy.
2. She looks a bit like her mother.
3. What's your new boss like?
4. Are you like your brother?
5. Do you like your brother?

7 If you have Student's Cassette B, find Unit 16, Lesson C, Listening Exercise 2. Listen to the recording and try to write down three or more sentences.

8 ▭ Read this with a dictionary.

IT'S A LONG STORY
15

Judy ran downstairs and into the dining room. No Jasper – only the ghost. 'Can I help you?' he asked politely. 'Would you like some breakfast?' 'Where's Jasper?' asked Judy. 'He's gone out,' said the ghost. 'Oh dear,' said Judy. 'Lend me a pen and paper, could you?'
   Quickly she wrote a note to Jasper:
     'Dear Jasper,
     It was wonderful. But I have to go. I'm sorry. I wanted
     to say goodbye to you, but perhaps it is better like this.
     Thank you for a beautiful memory.
     Judy.'
   She said goodbye to the ghost, who looked sad, and walked out of the castle. Not far along the road there was a bus stop. If she could get to Inverness before lunch, she could catch the afternoon plane to London and buy some new clothes before catching the night flight to Rio. Tomorrow morning she could be in Sam's arms. How wonderful! Judy started crying.
   At the bus stop, Judy read the timetable. Buses for Inverness ran every three hours, but she was lucky – there was one in twenty minutes. As she stood waiting, she looked out over the lake. A few hundred yards away there was a man fishing in a boat. She could hear him singing in the clear still air. He had a wonderful voice – a voice that Judy recognised – and he was singing an old Scottish love song. It was Jasper. Tears came into Judy's eyes, and she looked away from the boat, up into the peaceful sky. High above Loch Ness, a golden eagle was flying in circles. There were pretty little clouds looking like splashes of white paint against the deep blue. And two parachutes.

THERE IS NO PRACTICE BOOK WORK FOR LESSON 16D.

Unit 17 Ordering and asking

17A I'll have roast beef

1 Change *not any* to *no*; change *no* to *not any*.
Examples:

There isn't any beer.

There's no beer.

I've got no friends.

I haven't got any friends.

1. There are no more potatoes.
2. There isn't any tea in the pot.
3. I didn't spend any money yesterday. (I spent . . .)
4. Fifty million years ago there were no people.
5. There aren't any good films on TV this evening.
6. We haven't got any food in the house.

2 Complete the restaurant conversations.

CUSTOMER 1: .... table .... four?
WAITER: Yes, just over here, madam.

* * *

C1: .... tomato salad, please, and then ....
fish.
W: ...., sir?
C2: .... soup, and .... roast beef with a
green salad.

* * *

W: .... drink?
C1: .... lager, please.
C2: .... give .... lager, ...?
W: .... course, sir.

* * *

C1: .... beef?
C2: .... fish?
C1: Very good. .... potatoes aren't very nice,
....

* * *

W: .... everything ....?
C1: Yes, fine, thank you.

* * *

W: .... a little more coffee?
C1: No, ...
C2: Yes, ...

* * *

C1: .... bill, please?
W: ....
C1: .... service ....?
W: Yes, madam.

3 Use your dictionary. Find out the names of these things and learn them.

4 If you have Student's Cassette B, find Unit 17, Lesson A, Exercise 3. First listen and try to remember the answers. Then write down three or more of the questions and answers.

"Steak too tough, sir?"

5 These are extracts from diaries written by adolescent boys (boys from about twelve to about sixteen years old) in London. The first time you read them, use a dictionary to look up the <u>underlined</u> words.

'I got up and had sausage, egg, bacon and tomatoes for breakfast and read the *Sunday Mirror*. Then my brother Wally knocked at the door. He asked me if I wanted to go fishing with him and June, my sister-in-law. I quickly got my boots on and went with them in their van. We got to Broxbourne about 12.30 and Wally and me started fishing and June started getting the dinner with a calor gas cooker. We had sausage, egg and bacon again, after that a cup of hot orange and a piece of swiss roll. Then it started to rain. It poured down and we all got <u>soaked</u>, so we made for home. When we got back they came in and Mum made us a hot cup of tea. Then Wally and June went off home.'

Today I got up at eight o'clock and went swimming with my uncle. We got to the York Hall baths at nine. There were not many people in there. We fooled around and had a <u>couple</u> of <u>races</u>; I <u>lost</u> both. We came out at 10.30 and I came home.'

'My <u>cousin</u> and I took the dog out for a walk at 10.15. We stayed out quite a long while looking for girls.'

'I had my tea, washed and left for the girl-friend's house. When I arrived her mother let me in and told me to take a seat in the living-room. We watched television for most of the evening.'

8.30 p.m. My <u>fiancée</u> came round. We went to see my nan*, who lives in the same flats as me. We always have a good laugh when we go to see her, and my girl loves hearing her talk about the people she meets in the <u>market</u> every day.'

'About half past seven I went round my fiancée's flat, and sat down with her mum and dad and had a talk with them. We watched television for a while and then all went out for a drink.'

nan: grandmother

(from *Adolescent Boys of East London* by Peter Wilmott)

"We'd like a table near a waiter . . ."

"How can you say it was very nice? You slept through most of it."

17B Could you lend me some sugar?

1 Can you complete the following sentences *without looking* at the Student's Book?

1. '................. .... trouble .... lend ....
   .... tea?'
   '................., of ....'
2. '................. me. .... got .... light, ...?'
   'Just ....'
3. 'Have .... cigarette?'
   '................., don't ....'
4. '................. .... dictionary?'
   '................. afraid .... got ....'

2 Polite or casual? What can you say if you want to:

1. Borrow your teacher's car for the weekend?
2. Borrow £1 from your best friend?
3. Borrow your father's favourite jacket?
4. Get a cigarette from somebody that you don't know?
5. Get a cigarette from your sister?

How can you say 'No' when:

6. Your teacher wants to borrow your car?
7. Your brother wants to borrow your pencil?
8. A friend wants to borrow some milk, but you haven't got any?

3 *Lend* or *borrow*? Put the correct verb, in the correct form, in each blank.

1. Could you possibly .... me $20 for a day or two?
2. I .... my mother's car yesterday, and I lost the keys.
3. Could I .... that pencil for a moment?
4. Ann always .... me her flat when I go to Paris.
5. I'm sorry to trouble you, but could I .... an egg, please?

4 Match the rooms and the verbs.

Example: 6C

1. kitchen   a. wash
2. bedroom   b. sit and relax
3. bathroom   c. keep a car
4. living room   d. sleep
5. dining room   e. cook
6. garage   f. eat

Now make sentences. Example:

You can keep a car in a garage.

5 If you have Student's Cassette B, find Unit 17, Lesson B, Exercise 2 (only sentences 1 to 5 are recorded here). Read each sentence with correct stress and intonation. Then check with the recording.

1. Sorry to **trouble you,** but could you **lend** me some **bread?**
2. Could you **lend** me a dictionary?
3. Could you **show** me some **black sweaters, please?**
4. **Excuse** me. **Have** you got a light, please?
5. Could you **possibly lend** me your **car** for **half** an **hour?**

6 Quick crossword. You can use your dictionary.

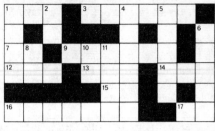

ACROSS

1. Between hip and foot.
3. .... me, have you got a light?
7. I'm sorry, there's .... more roast beef.
9. Just a ....
12. Not wet.
13. You drive it.
14. You see with it.
15. My name .... George.
16. I'm sorry to .... you.
17. United Kingdom.

DOWN

1. Could you .... me your umbrella, please?
2. I .... to work by bus.
4. 'Could I borrow your dictionary?' 'Yes, of ....'
5. You usually do this at night.
6. Do you .... English?
8. Have you got any brothers .... sisters?
10. She's a very n..e person.
11. At the end of your finger.

(Solution on page 132.)

78

17C   Somewhere different

1 Complete these conversations.

A: Excuse me. Where can I buy a colour film near here?

B: ....

A: Thanks anyway.

*   *   *

A: ....?

B: At the supermarket.

A: ....?

B: First right, second left.

A: ....?

B: About two hundred yards.

A: ....

B: You're welcome.

*   *   *

SALLY: ....

BRUCE: Hello. Could I speak to Lorna, please?

SALLY: .... Can I take a message?

BRUCE: No, it's all right. I'll ring back later.

SALLY: OK. ....

BRUCE: ....

*   *   *

A: .... go to the cinema tonight.

B: No, let's .... theatre.

A: No, it's too far.

B: OK. Why .... go and see Mother?

A: No. Look, ... we stay ....
home and .... TV?

B: Good idea. OK.

2 Put in the right preposition.

1. We're leaving here .... three days.
2. I had a drink with Peter .... Tuesday.
3. I usually work .... nine o'clock .... five.
4. This is a picture of my family .... holiday.
5. We spent three weeks .... the mountains.
6. I'm getting up .... six o'clock tomorrow.
7. I'm driving .... Scotland.
8. I'm staying with friends in Edinburgh ....
   four days.
9. I don't like travelling .... train.
10. 'Can you help me?'   'Yes, ... course.'

3 If you have Student's Cassette B, find Unit 17, Lesson C, Exercise 1 (only the first part of the conversation is recorded here). Listen and write down as much as you can.

"Artie, how would you pack if you were going to Mars?"

"Somewhere with no irregular verbs."

4 Read this with a dictionary and answer the questions.

A DREAM

Last night I had a strange dream. I was in a world where all the colours were different. The grass was orange, the trees were white; in the green sky there was a purple sun and a moon the colour of blood. I was a child again, eight years old, and I was lost. I felt very frightened and unhappy. In front of me there was a long street, stretching away as far as I could see. There were no people, but all around me I heard the noise of big insects. It was terribly hot. Suddenly a door opened on my left. I went into the house and ran up the stairs. When I got to the top, I saw a field full of blue horses. I called one of them; he came over to me and I got on his back. I don't know how far he took me – we went through forests, across rivers, past high mountains covered with black snow. At last we came to a town. The streets were full of people dressed in red. Nobody spoke. I said goodbye to my horse and walked until I came to a church. Inside I heard my mother's voice. I pushed the door, but it was too big and heavy – I couldn't move it. I called as loud as I could, but nothing happened. Then, very slowly, the door opened. In the church there were hundreds of people, all looking at me. They started to come towards me, slowly at first, then faster and faster . . . Then I woke up.

1. Do you think this was a true dream?
2. Do you like it?
3. Do you ever have dreams like this?

17D Meet me at eight

1 Pronunciation. Say the sentences with the correct stress.

1. **What** are you **do**ing this **eve**ning?
2. Would you **like** to **come** to the **cin**ema **with** me?
3. **How** a**bout** to**mor**row?
4. We're **leav**ing on **Mon**day.
5. **Just** for **two days.**
6. **Back** on Friday **night.**
7. The **chil**dren are **go**ing to **Moth**er.

2 Vocabulary revision. Do you know all these words and expressions? Can you pronounce them? Check in your dictionary if you're not sure.

window; table; minute; month; mountain; lunch; supper; give; bring; start; cost; meet; tell; different; sorry; next; tonight; tomorrow; perhaps; everything; Would you like . . . ?; of course; How about . . . ?; I'm afraid . . .

3 Translate these into your language.

1. Have you got a table for two?
2. I'll start with soup, please.
3. Is everything all right?
4. Would you like a little more coffee?
5. Could you bring us the bill, please?
6. Is service included?
7. Sorry to trouble you, but could you lend me some bread?
8. Could you possibly lend me your car for half an hour?
9. Could I borrow your umbrella?
10. Why don't we go to California for our holiday this year?
11. Hey, wait a minute. Let's think about this.
12. I think it's a good idea.
13. Let's catch a plane to Spain.

4 Complete the story with these words.

got into	kissed	understand	when	saw
woke up	then	didn't	sing	difficult
road	drive	fast	night	couldn't

A DREAM

Last .... I dreamt that I was in a very ....
car, driving along a road in Ireland. It was raining,
and I .... see very well. Then suddenly I ....
a woman standing in the middle of the ....
.... I stopped, she .... the car and told me
to .... to Dublin. It was .... to .... her,
because she had a strange accent. She started to
..............., and .... she looked at me and smiled. I
asked her name, but she .... answer. She smiled
again, and .... me on the cheek. Then I ....

5 Write the story of a dream (about 100 words).
Use some of these words and expressions (look at
page 80 to see how they are used).

I had a strange dream   I felt very frightened
in front of me   all around me   suddenly
I saw   there was   he/she came over to me
nothing happened   very slowly
faster and faster   I woke up

6 🔲 Read this with a dictionary.

Sam and Detective Sergeant Honeybone hit the water
together. Sam went under and came up. 'Help!' he
shouted, going under again. 'I can't swim!' he shouted, as
he came up again and went under for the third time.
Sam's life passed in front of his eyes as he went down,
down, down into the green water. His childhood in
London. Visiting his mother and father in prison. His first
girlfriend. His first bank robbery. Judy. Judy. He would
never see her again.

'Don't worry, you lovely man,' called Detective
Sergeant Honeybone. 'I'm an Olympic 400-metre gold
medallist.' She swam over to him with beautiful strong
strokes, caught him under the arms as he came up
again, and started pulling him towards the boat.

'Hello, Isabel,' said Jasper as they pulled Sam out of
the water. 'What are you doing here? And why have you
got Sam with you? He's the last person I want to see.'
'It's a long story,' said Detective Sergeant Honeybone. 'I'll
tell you later. Wait while I give Sam the kiss of life.' 'I
don't need the kiss of life,' said Sam. 'Oh yes you do,'
said Detective Sergeant Honeybone.

'All right,' said Jasper. 'I suppose we'd better go back
to the castle and find you some dry clothes. Pity. I was
hoping for a quiet morning's fishing.' He rowed the boat
over to the bank of the loch and they got out. Detective
Sergeant Honeybone picked up Sam in her beautiful
strong arms and they started walking down the road
towards the castle. As they passed the bus stop, Jasper
walked over to Judy, who was staring up at the sky.
'Good morning, you beautiful creature,' he said. 'Going
shopping? Don't forget lunch is at 12.30.' Judy turned her
back, tears streaming down her face. 'Don't talk to me
about lunch,' she said. 'I'm going to Rio to see Sam.' 'But
Sam's here,' said Jasper. 'Don't try to talk me out of it,'
said Judy. 'I've made up my mind, and I . . . what did you
say?' She turned round and looked across the road.
There was Detective Sergeant Honeybone, standing with
a soft smile on her lips looking down at Sam, who was
lying in her arms with his eyes closed. Judy's mouth fell
open.

Unit 18 More about the past

18A Where was Galileo born?

1 Make 'follow-up' questions.

1. Amelia Earhart took flying lessons when she was 22. (*Where . . . ?*)

   Where did she take lessons?
2. Galileo discovered sunspots. (*When . . . ?*)
3. Marie Curie was born in Warsaw. (*When . . . ?*)
4. Ho Chi Minh once went to New York. (*How . . . ?*)
5. Amelia Earhart once worked for the Red Cross. (*Where . . . ?*)
6. Galileo's lectures were very famous. (*Why . . . ?*)
7. Marie and Pierre Curie had a famous daughter. (*What . . . ?*)

2 Make negative sentences.

1. Shakespeare wrote plays. (*novels*)

   Shakespeare did not write novels.
2. Dickens wrote novels. (*paint pictures*)
3. Van Gogh painted pictures. (*play football*)
4. Maradona played football. (*live in London*)
5. Karl Marx lived in London. (*New York*)
6. John Lennon lived in New York. (*travel to the moon*)
7. Neil Armstrong travelled to the moon. (*write plays*)

3 If you have Student's Cassette B, find Unit 18, Lesson A, Exercise 3 (only the second section is recorded here). Listen to the recording and see how much you can write down. Then practise saying some of the sentences.

4 Read the first text and its notes. Then read the second text and write notes for it.

Margareta Gertruida Zelle was born in Leeuwarden, in the Netherlands, in 1876. She married an army officer and went with him to Indonesia, where she learnt Javanese and Hindu dances. She went back to Europe, where she became a famous dancer, calling herself 'Mata Hari'. She was accused of being a spy for the Germans and was executed in Vincennes, in France, in 1917.

Margareta Gertruida Zelle (called 'Mata Hari')
– Dutch dancer
– Leeuwarden, 1876 – Vincennes, 1917
– husband: army officer
– learnt Javanese & Hindu dances in Indonesia
– back to Europe: famous
– executed as a German spy

Marco Polo was born in Venice in 1254. With his father and his uncle, who were businessmen, he travelled to China in 1275. They were the first Europeans to do this. Marco Polo stayed at the court of the Chinese emperor for many years, and went as an ambassador for the emperor to Tonkin, Annam, India and Persia. He went back to Venice in 1295, made rich by his travels. Polo wrote a book about his experiences, but not many people believed him at first. He died in 1324.

5 Write about someone from your country's history.
OR: Write a short paragraph about your mother/grandfather *etc.* as a child.

18B America invades Britain!

1 What are the infinitives of these past verbs? Example:

went *go*

began   bought   broke
brought   fought   knew
left   saw   thought   told
took   woke

2 Put irregular past verbs into the sentences. (More than one answer is sometimes possible.)

1. He .... to school in a very small village.
2. I .... home very late last night.
3. Charlie Chaplin .... seven children.
4. The teacher .... some photos to show us yesterday.
5. He .... he was sorry, but she .... that he wasn't.
6. I .... an aspirin half an hour ago, and my head's much better now.
7. She sat on her glasses and .... them.
8. Yehudi Menuhin .... playing the violin when he was very young.
9. He had a few minutes with nothing to do, so he .... a cake.

3 Put one of these into each sentence. (You can use the words more than once, and more than one answer is sometimes possible.)

and	as soon as	because	but	finally
first of all	next	so	that	then
where	who	why		

1. I had a cup of tea and .... went straight to bed.
2. The party went on for a long time, but the last people .... went home at 5.00.
3. Could you ask her to phone me .... she comes home?
4. .... I'd like tomato salad; then I'd like steak; and after that I'll have coffee.
5. I couldn't phone her .... she hasn't got a phone.
6. I don't know .... she hasn't got a phone.
7. I was very tired, ... I went upstairs to lie down.
8. We've got a small house in the mountains .... we go in the holidays.
9. .... she studied music; .... she spent two years working in New York; .... she got married and had two children; and .... she started a computer business in San Francisco.
10. I love you .... I want to marry you.
11. I love you .... I don't want to marry you.
12. I knew .... he wasn't happy.
13. I've got some good friends .... live in Brisbane.

4 Say these words with the right stress.

finally American everything century
university history because

5 Vocabulary revision. How many words can you add to this list?

shy, optimistic, . . .

6 Read these sentences; you can use a dictionary. Then put the sentences in order, to make two paragraphs of a story.

But Florence found parties boring; she wanted to be a nurse.
Then she was in charge of a nursing-home for women in London.
Florence Nightingale came from a rich family and was very pretty.
Finally, in 1850, when she was 30, her parents accepted her decision.
In her family, young girls usually spent their time going to parties until they married rich young men.
Soon she was asked to go to the Crimea to take charge of the wounded soldiers.
So she went to study in a hospital in Germany.

* * *

Forty per cent of the patients died.
By 1900 unsafe hospitals and ignorant nurses were things of the past.
The death rate dropped to two per cent.
The conditions in the Crimean hospital were terrible.
Workmen put in a proper drainage system and supplied pure drinking water.
Certain beds seemed fatal: soldiers died in them after two days.
She was an important force in the movement to reform hospitals and nursing in England.
On her return to England people greeted Florence Nightingale as a heroine.
Nightingale decided that this was because of bad drains, and insisted that the government do something about it.

18C   Who? What? Which? How? Where? When?

1 Write the infinitives of twenty verbs you know. Do you know the past tense forms? Write them down if you do; if you don't, look them up in the dictionary and write down what you learn.

INFINITIVE	PAST TENSE
go	went

2 Write the text with capital letters and punctuation. (Begin: *On the night of April . . .*) Then look on page 89 of the Student's Book and check your answer.

on the night of april 24 1778 captain john paul jones quietly brought his ship ranger to whitehaven in the north-west of england as soon as he arrived he took a group of his men to one of the inns in the town broke into it and had a drink with them then they started work first of all they went to the fort and destroyed the guns next they began burning british ships the british sailors woke up and started fighting against the americans but they could not stop jones and his men

3 Put in *a/an*, *the* or – (= no article).

1. She was .... first woman to fly across .... Atlantic.
2. He was .... student at .... Columbia University.
3. I'm .... tallest in .... my family.
4. York is in .... north-east of .... England.
5. She looks like .... actress, but actually she's .... housewife.
6. What was .... name of .... man who discovered penicillin?
7. Who starred in .... film .... *Third Man*?
8. I play .... football every Saturday.
9. .... books are very expensive.

4 Practise saying these words with the correct stress.

animal   disagree   famous
across   about   member
novel   discover   football
expensive

5 Choose the correct form.

1. How | did Blériot travel | to England?
      | travelled Blériot |
      | did travel Blériot |

2. When | started the war?
        | did start the war?
        | did the war start?

3. Why | she left?
       | she did leave?
       | did she leave?

4. Where | did you go?
         | you went?

5. What | did want your mother?
        | did your mother want?
        | your mother wanted?

6. When | was born Shakespeare?
        | was Shakespeare born?
        | Shakespeare was born?

7. Who | did write | *Hamlet*?
       | wrote |

8. What | happened | yesterday?
        | did happen |

6 Do the crossword.

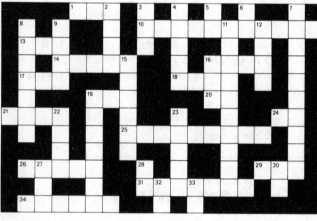

ACROSS

1. The British sailors started fighting, ... they could not stop Jones and his men.
10. 'Was that television programme ....?' 'No, I fell asleep after ten minutes.'
13. How long .... did he leave?
14. I can pronounce a lot of words that I can't ...., and I can .... a lot of words that I can't pronounce.
16. I'm tired, and I'd like to go ....
17. Past tense of *get*.
18. The new telephones are smaller .... the old ones.
19. I .... cook quite well, but I don't enjoy it.
20. Present tense of *did*.
21. Past tense of *go*.
24. I'm not quite .... tall .... my boyfriend.
25. The cooker was ...., but it cooks much better than the cheaper ones.
26. I always .... with a window open.

29. Present tense of *said*.
31. My cousins .... got here at ten o'clock in the evening – their plane was four hours late.
34. His office is on the first floor, up the .... and to the right.

DOWN

2. Present tense of *told*.
3. 'When .... you leave school?' 'In 1975.'
4. When did you .... learning English?
5. Is your brother dark .... fair?
6. The same .... *24 across*.
7. She's a student at Yale ....
8. In 1778, the British .... at the American navy.
9. .... people like music.
11. My car's very fast, bit it's not very ....: it uses a lot of petrol.
12. First she phoned her boyfriend, and .... she made some coffee.
15. Judy's hair is much .... than it was the last time I saw her.
16. Past tense of *have*.
19. Oh, look! This one's much .... It's only £1.50.
22. I can .... faster than I can write.
23. Past tense of *begin*.
27. We've got a .... of bread, but we haven't got much cheese.
28. What was the name .... the man who built the Eiffel Tower?
30. What were you doing .... ten o'clock last night?
32. Nairobi is the biggest city .... Kenya.
33. 'Who's the oldest person here?' 'I ....'

(Solution on page 133.)

18D Washed and shaved, had breakfast

1 Which words have the strongest stress in these sentences? Mark the stress and then practise saying the sentences. Example:

He says he's twenty-six, but he's only twenty-one.

1. I asked for orange juice, not tomato juice.
2. 'Is that Peter?' 'No, this is John.'
3. I don't like yellow. Have you got anything in red?
4. Tuesday's no good. Can we meet on Thursday?
5. French bread is much nicer than English bread.
6. French bread is nice, but French milk isn't always very good.

2 Make at least ten sentences from this table. Use *neither*, *both* and *but*.

NAME	PLAYS FOOTBALL	LIKES BEER	READS NOVELS	IS INTERESTED IN POLITICS	GOES TO CHURCH	GOES CAMPING
Robert	No	Yes	No	Yes	No	Yes
Janet	Yes	No	Yes	No	Yes	No
Kevin	Yes	Yes	Yes	No	No	No
Philip	Yes	Yes	No	No	No	Yes
Sue	No	Yes	No	Yes	Yes	Yes

Examples: Robert neither plays football nor reads novels.

Neither Robert nor Sue plays football.

Janet and Kevin both read novels.

OR: Both Janet and Kevin ...

Sue goes to church, but Philip doesn't.

3 Put in *tell*, *tells*, *told*, *say*, *says* or *said*.

1. Al .... the policeman that he got up at eight.
2. Jake .... that he met Al at 12.30.
3. Do you always .... people what you really think?
4. I saw Ann yesterday, and she .... that she didn't want to come with us.
5. Today's newspaper .... that the weather will be fine all day.
6. My brother David never .... me when he's coming to see me.
7. Kate .... me that she didn't know what to do.
8. I .... that I wanted to go back home.
9. Some people .... that Mary is very intelligent, but I don't think so.

4 Vocabulary revision. Do you know all these words and expressions? Can you pronounce them? Check in your dictionary if you're not sure.

Europe; job; money; place; world; football match; life; size; town; help; meet; remember; study; want; show; get up; wake up; shave; have breakfast/lunch; wear; buy; free; strong; first; enough; quietly; late.

5 Translate these into your language.

1. Galileo was born in the 16th century.
2. She was the first woman to fly a plane across the Atlantic.
3. What was the name of the man who discovered penicillin?
4. Students came from all over Europe to hear his lectures.
5. What sport was Pele famous for?
6. I got up, washed, shaved and had breakfast.
7. He told the policeman that he got up at eight o'clock, but actually he got up at ten o'clock.
8. It's not true.
9. Both Al and Jake went to bed late.
10. Neither Al nor Jake went to a football match.

6 If you have Student's Cassette B, find Unit 18, Lesson D, Exercise 2. Listen to Al's statement and try to write down some of the things he says.

7 🔊 **Read this with a dictionary.**

JUDY: Who is that woman?

JASPER: May I introduce my sister Isabel? Isabel, this is Judy.

SAM: If you're Jasper's sister, why is your name Honeybone?

ISABEL: It's a long story. Give me a kiss, Sam.

JUDY: Put that man down at once.

JASPER: Ladies, . . .

ISABEL: Who is that woman, and why is she wearing my sweater?

JUDY: Sam, get down.

ISABEL: He's not feeling very strong.

JUDY: That's all right. I'm a medical student. I'll look after him.

ISABEL: Oh, no. You're not playing doctors with my Sam.

JASPER: Ladies, . . .

JUDY: He's not your Sam. He's my Sam.

ISABEL: Take my sweater off at once.

JASPER: Ladies, please.

JUDY: ⎫
ISABEL: ⎬ Shut up.

JUDY: Sam, protect me from this mad woman.

ISABEL: It's all right, Sam. Don't pay any attention to her. I'll look after you.

JASPER: Sam, where are you going?

JUDY: ⎫
ISABEL: ⎬ Sam, come back!

(Splash!)

"Where'd you get this newspaper, boy? It's in French!"

Unit 19 Getting to know you

19A Is this seat free?

1 Complete the conversations.

A: .... seat ....?
B: No, ... it ....

*   *   *

A: .... car?
B: Sorry, ... need ....

*   *   *

A: .... mind .... look at .... newspaper?
B: .... all.

*   *   *

A: .... borrow .... pen?
B: .... course.

2 Some of these words are pronounced with the vowel /iː/, like *eat*. Some of them are pronounced with /ɪ/, like *it*. Some are pronounced with neither /iː/ nor /ɪ/. Say the words, and then write them in three groups according to the pronunciation.

please   live   five   give   green   pol*i*ce   d*i*nner   friend

sing   s*i*ster   ski   this   these   fine   people   him

jeans   bread   Engl*a*nd   pr*e*tt*y*   steak   fridge   meat   meet

feel   speak   cheap

GROUP 1 (like *eat*)	GROUP 2 (like *it*)	GROUP 3 (other)
please	live	five
green	give	friend
police	dinner	

3 Write ten sentences.

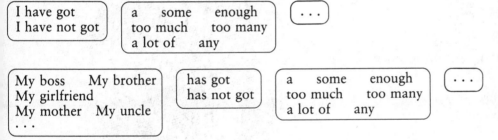

I have got / I have not got	a some enough / too much too many / a lot of any	(. . .)

My boss My brother / My girlfriend / My mother My uncle / . . .	has got / has not got	a some enough / too much too many / a lot of any	(. . .)

4 If you have Student's Cassette B, find Unit 19, Lesson A, Exercise 4 (only the first six requests are recorded here). Listen to the requests; refuse, and then give permission.

5 Read this text; if necessary, look up the underlined words in a dictionary. (The writer is talking about a time during the Second World War, when he was hiding from the Germans in an Italian hospital.)

Then the *superiora*, the head of the hospital, appeared, a middle-aged woman with a gentle, resolute face. She was carrying a large tray loaded with tea things and bread and butter, ginger biscuits and raspberry jam. I tried to thank her, partly in French, partly with the few Italian words I knew, but they got mixed up with bits of school Latin, and then I ran out of words completely and looked at her in despair, and she smiled and went out of the room and came back with the girl I had met in the farmyard that morning.

She was wearing a white, open-necked shirt and a blue cotton skirt. She was brown, she was slim, she had good legs, she had ash blonde hair and blue eyes and she had a fine nose. When she smiled she looked saucy, and when she didn't she looked serious. She was all right.

'You have not forgotten me?' she said. I assured her that I had not done so.

'My mother has made an *apfelstrudel* for you,' she said. 'In my country we call them *struklji*. We are not Italian. We are Slovenes. You can eat it after your dinner. Tonight you have chicken. The *superiora* told me. Be kind to her and do what she says. Now I must go. I have to take food to your friends.'

I asked her when she would come again.

'I will come tomorrow, if the *superiora* allows. If you want I will teach you Italian. It will be useful for you, and you can teach me English. I speak badly. My name is Wanda.'

(from *Love and War in the Apennines* by Eric Newby – adapted)

19B How often do you come here?

1 Put in *always, usually, very often, often, quite often, sometimes, occasionally, hardly ever, never.*

1. It .... rains in Britain.
2. People .... get up late on Sundays.
3. Women .... win the Nobel prize.
4. Good-looking people .... have nice personalities.
5. Policemen .... smile.
6. Politicians .... tell the truth.
7. Women .... give flowers to men.
8. Elephants .... eat meat.
9. Passport photographs .... look like the people.
10. People .... live to be 100 years old.
11. Holidays .... cost too much money.

2 How often do you:

go to the theatre?   travel by bus?   dance?
drink wine?   play tennis?   go swimming?
go to church?   listen to the radio?
write letters?   drive a car?

Examples:

I travel by bus twice a day.

I play tennis every Saturday.

3 Write 'reply questions' to answer the following sentences. ('*Are you?*' '*Is it?*' etc.)

1. I work on Saturday mornings.
2. Kumiko speaks beautiful French.
3. I like swimming.
4. Andrew eats like a horse.
5. My father's got a flat in North London.
6. I've got a new car.
7. Robert came to see us yesterday.
8. Your sister looks like you.
9. You're very beautiful.

4 Complete the sentences.

1. My mother likes skiing, and so .... I.
2. All my friends can dance, but I ....
3. 'I've got a new dress.' 'That's funny. So ....'
4. 'I'm Capricorn.' 'So ....'
5. 'I'm tired.' '............... not.'
6. 'My brother can speak six languages.' 'So .... I.'
7. 'Where do you live?' 'Oxford.' 'That's funny. So .... I.'
8. 'I like smoked salmon.' 'Oh, I .... at all.'

5 If you have Student's Cassette B, find Unit 19, Lesson B, Exercise 3 (only the second set of sentences is recorded here). Listen and make 'reply questions' ('*Did you?*' etc.).

"Good morning. Now that was what I call a real party."

19C What do you think of . . . ?

1 What (or who) is your favourite song/sport/country/town/drink/food/painter/composer/season/writer? (Write at least five sentences.) Example:

My favourite sport is cycling

2 Answer these questions.

1. Do you like horses?
2. What do you think of golf?
3. Do you like poetry?
4. Do you like Western films?
5. Do you like cats?
6. Have you ever been to the opera?
7. Have you always lived where you live now?
8. Have you ever seen the film *Casablanca*?
9. Have you always liked the same sort of music as you like now?
10. Have you ever met anyone famous?

3 Make questions.

1. ever Africa to been you have ?

   <u>Have you ever been</u>

   <u>to Africa ?</u>

2. Tokyo you always lived have in ?
3. before you Rome been have to ?
4. seen Russian you films ever any have ?
5. novel have tried ever you write to a ?
6. plane have ever you a been on ?
7. driven before you bus ever have a ?

4 Say these sentences, and then put them in groups according to the rhythm.

Where are you from?   John's a nice man.   There were two cars.
How do you do?   Buy a large steak.   Do you live here?
First on the left.   Not the green one.   English and French.
In a red car.   Do you like fish?   Thirty-five days.
What do you want?

GROUP 1   GROUP 2   GROUP 3

☐☐☐☐   ☐☐☐☐   **?**

<u>Where are you from?</u>   <u>John's a nice man.</u>   ....

<u>How do you do?</u>   ....

"You know, most people's favourite number is 7, but mine is 6273990103648829910048253048103855722295710049."

19D   I've only known her for twenty-four hours, but . . .

1 Can you remember the past tense forms? Copy and complete the table and learn the past participles of the irregular verbs.

INFINITIVE	PAST TENSE	PAST PARTICIPLE
Regular verbs		
live	lived	lived
work	worked	worked
start	....	....
stop	....	....
play	....	....
change	....	....
Irregular verbs		
be	....	been
know	....	known
have	....	had
see	....	seen
read (/riːd/)	....	read (/red/)
write	....	written
hear (/hɪə(r)/)	....	heard (/hɜːd/)

2 Complete the sentences with past participles.

1. Have you ever .... *Carmen*?
2. How long have you .... married?
3. How long have you .... my friend Andrew?
4. How long have you .... that car?
5. Have you ever .... to Scotland?
6. Have you ever .... any of Agatha Christie's detective stories?
7. Have you ever .... Beethoven's First Symphony?
8. Have you ever .... a poem? (*write*)

89

3 Put in the correct verb form.

1. Where .... you ....? (*live*)
2. How long .... you .... there? (*live*)
3. .... you .... my friend Alison Haynes? (*know*)
4. How long .... you .... her? (*know*)
5. How long .... you .... that watch? (*have*)
6. .... you .... today's newspaper? (*read*)
7. .... you .... Mary today? (*see*)
8. What .... you .... of your new boss? (*think*)
9. How long .... you .... learning English? (*be*)
10. Why .... you learning English? (*be*)

4 Translate these into your language.

1. Is this seat free?
2. 'Do you mind if I sit here?'   'Not at all. Please do.'
3. I'd rather you didn't.
4. I always come here on Sunday mornings.
5. Oh, do you? So do I.
6. I go to the theatre about every six weeks.
7. She goes skiing twice a year.
8. What do you think of the government?
9. Have you always lived in London?
10. Have you ever been to Africa?
11. for 24 hours; since yesterday
12. How long have you lived here?
13. How long have you been learning English?

5 Vocabulary revision. Do you know all these words and expressions? Can you pronounce them? Check in your dictionary if you're not sure.

paper; window; day; week; month; year; TV; holiday; letter; place; music; look at; sit; smoke; watch; ski; come; think; cold; free; terrible; beautiful; sure; interested in; actually; every; often; sometimes; always; really; only; please; not bad.

6 Read this with a dictionary.

IT'S A LONG STORY
18

'North-east Highlands Police Control, calling all cars. Calling all cars. The hijackers of the Boeing 707 from Rio are believed to be in the Loch Ness area after leaving the plane by parachute about twenty minutes ago. Proceed at once to the vicinity of Castle Clandonald and begin searching.
    Description as follows:
Man, British, medium height, dark hair, small moustache, small brown eyes, wearing a blue suit and black shoes. He is believed to be Sam Watson, who is wanted in connection with a series of bank robberies. He is carrying a gun, and may be dangerous. Woman, nationality unknown, tall, blonde, blue eyes, attractive, athletic build, wearing dark clothes and shoes. Nothing is known about her identity.
    Approach these people with caution. Repeat, approach with caution.'

"Have you been waiting long, Sir?"

Unit 20 Consolidation

20A Things to remember: Units 17, 18 and 19

1 Make sentences with *neither . . . nor*, as in the examples.

I am not tall and I am not short.
I am neither tall nor short.
Alex does not speak French and Rose does not speak French.
Neither Alex nor Rose speaks French.

1. I am not fair and I am not dark.
2. She is not at home and she is not in her office.
3. John is not fat, but he is not slim.
4. It is not true and it is not false.
5. I do not speak German and I do not speak French.
6. Our village has not got a bank or a post office.
7. John is not married and Peter is not married.
8. My mother does not smoke and my father does not smoke.

2 Make five or more sentences with *neither . . . nor* about yourself and other people.

3 Put in the right verbs.

1. 'I'm tired.' 'So .... I.'
2. 'Alice was very bad-tempered yesterday.' 'So .... Bill.'
3. 'We've never been to Australia.' 'Oh, we .... – three times.'
4. 'Lucy can speak five languages.' 'So .... Joe.'
5. 'Eric wants to be a doctor.' 'Oh, ... he?'
6. 'I think it's terrible.' 'So .... I.'
7. 'We went to Wales last weekend.' '............... you really? Was it nice?'
8. 'I like all her films.' 'Oh, I .... I think they're very bad.'

4 Vocabulary revision. Can you put in the missing nouns and adjectives? Can you add some yourself?

NOUN	ADJECTIVE
Europe	European
America	American
Asia	....
....	African
Australia	....
....	English
Ireland	....
....	Scottish
Wales	....
France	....
Germany	....
....	Spanish
....	Italian
Poland	....
Turkey	....
....	Greek
....	Brazilian
....	Mexican
Egypt	....
....	Israeli
Nigeria	....
Japan	....
....	Chinese

5 Write suitable replies to these sentences.

1. I'm hungry.
   Would you like a sandwich?
2. I'm thirsty.
3. I'm bored.
4. I'm tired.
5. I'm unhappy.
6. How often do you go to the cinema?
7. I slept badly last night.
8. I can speak three languages.
9. Could you possibly lend me your car?
10. Let's have a drink.
11. Why don't we go and see a film?
12. Do you mind if I look at your paper?
13. What do you think of the government?
14. Do you like pop music?

6 What did you do yesterday evening?

7 Read this once without using a dictionary. Then read it again with a dictionary if you like.

If you are invited to an English home, at five o'clock in the morning you get a cup of tea. You must not say 'Go away'. On the contrary, you have to say, with your best five o'clock smile: 'Thank you so much. I love a cup of early morning tea, especially early in the morning.'

Then you have tea for breakfast; then you have tea at eleven o'clock in the morning; then after lunch; then you have tea for tea; then after supper; and again at eleven o'clock at night.

You must not refuse tea under the following circumstances: if it is hot; if it is cold; if you are tired; if anybody thinks that you might be tired; if you are nervous; if you are happy; before you go out; if you are out; if you have just returned home; if you have had no tea for some time; if you have just had a cup.

You definitely must not follow my example. I sleep at five o'clock in the morning; I have coffee for breakfast; I drink innumerable cups of black coffee during the day.

The other day, for instance, I wanted a cup of coffee and a piece of cheese for tea. It was a very hot day, and my wife made some cold coffee and put it in the refrigerator, where it froze* solid. On the other hand, she left the cheese on the kitchen table, where it melted. So I had a piece of coffee and a glass of cheese.

*past of *freeze*

(from *How to be an Alien* by George Mikes – adapted)

"I've spent 25 years making a name for myself and now you want me to CHANGE it?!"

20B Past, Perfect and Present

1 Find one or more suitable verbs to go with each noun. Example:

letter write read

tea   tennis   steak   music   TV   a car
a door   a train   money   dirty clothes
a book   a song   a piano   a house

2 Practise saying these words with the correct stress.

century   animal   radio   famous
wonderful   favourite   certainly   somewhere
finally   everything   cinema

idea   policeman   believe   important
together   already   tonight   occasionally

cigarette   disagree   university

"Haven't you seen anyone posting letters before?"

3 Choose the right tenses and write out the letter.

10 Bound Road
Wood Park
London SW17 6OJ
16.6.90

Dear Susan,

Thanks so much for your letter. It was lovely to hear from you again and to get all your news.

Things (*are starting / start*) to go very well. I (*have come / came*) to London in the first week of June, and (*have found / found*) a room the first day I was here. That was really lucky – some people (*are spending / spend*) ages looking for somewhere to live. It's a nice place in a big house. The landlady's really friendly, and there are a lot of other students. They (*came / come*) from all over the world, but most of them (*are speaking / speak*) good English, so it's easy to talk to them.

College is OK, but I think I (*change / 'm going to change*) from Design to Engineering – I (*'m / 've been*) interested in Engineering for a long time, and I really think it's the right thing for me. I (*'ve talked / talked*) to two or three of the teachers about it, and I (*'ve seen / saw*) the Principal yesterday, and they all say it's OK to change.

Social life is great! I (*'ve been / went*) out every night this week, and tomorrow I (*have / 'm having*) a party in my room for my new friends. Next weekend some of us (*go / are going*) to Wales – let's hope the weather's OK. I (*play / 'm playing*) tennis two or three times a week, too. The only problem is finding time to work!

When (*do you come / are you going to come*) over? It would be lovely to see you, and I'd really like you to meet some of my friends.

Tell Joe I (*haven't forgotten / didn't forget*) him, and I (*write / 'll write*) as soon as I can. And give my love to Alice and Ted and the others. And a big kiss to you. Write again soon.

Love,

Karen

4 Write a letter to an old friend. Use some of the words and expressions from Exercise 3.

5 Try the crossword.

ACROSS

1. It's .... I've only known him for 24 hours, but I feel we've known each other all our lives.
4. 'Do you like music?' '............... depends what sort of music.'
7. The opposite of *rich*.
8. *So do I = I do* ....
10. A place where people study.
12. My favourite colour.
13. 'You can't do it.' 'Yes, ...' (*Two words*)
14. The opposite of *late*.
16. Could you possibly .... me some sugar?
18. Not *your*, *his*, *her*, *our* or *their*.
19. *I do too = ... do I.*

DOWN

1. What's your .... colour?
2. More noisy.
3. The day before the day before tomorrow.
5. Pronounced the same as *8 across*, but spelt differently.
6. Take from one place to another in your hands.
7. Could I .... borrow your car?
9. Would you like something to eat .... drink?
11. You travel on these.
15. She studied .... London University.
17. 'I think she's nice.' 'Oh, ... you?'

(*Solution on page 133.*)

93

20C Choose

1 Copy and complete the table of irregular verbs.

INFINITIVE	PAST TENSE	PAST PARTICIPLE
fly	flew	flown
spend	....	....
show	....	....
find	....	....
catch	....	....
learn	....	....
pay	....	....
build	....	....
lead	....	....
feel	....	....

2 Put in *some more, any more, a little more* or *no more.*

1. 'Have you got .... chocolate?' 'I'm sorry, I haven't.'
2. Let me give you .... coffee.
3. 'Is there .... fish?' 'Yes, here you are.'
4. 'Here's your book back. Thanks very much.' 'I've got .... books by the same writer. Would you like to borrow them?'
5. There are .... mushrooms, but we've got some potatoes.
6. 'Can you lend me £5?' 'I haven't got .... money – I gave it all to you yesterday.'
7. 'Would you like anything more to eat or drink?' 'Just .... tea, please.'
8. I'm very hungry. Could I possibly have .... potatoes?

3 If you have Student's Cassette B, find Unit 20, Lesson C, Pronunciation Exercise 2. Listen to the recording and practise the pronunciation.

4 Read the text, choose the missing words from the box, and write them in order. (There is one word too many.)

'Don't move. ......1...... move.' The voice was calm, slow and deadly. 'Now throw your guns into the middle of the room. ......2...... That's right. Put your hands up and ......3...... back against the wall, nice and slow. Keep your hands up, lady. That's very good. Now turn round slowly and face the wall. And if you ......4...... to stay alive, just keep looking at that wall. You too, Mr Galvin.'

......5...... him, Galvin ......6...... a key turn in the door of the safe. He moved his head a little, looking at the reflection in his glasses. The big man was ......7...... with his back to them by the safe, ...8...... inside. With one smooth movement, Galvin turned and dived ......9...... the table; a moment later, the big man was ......10...... on the floor gasping for breath. Galvin picked up his gun and put it in his pocket. '......11...... them to ......12...... a younger man next time,' he said.

(From *A Gun for Your Money* by Neil MacShaw)

everybody	nobody	lying	standing
across	behind	get	heard	looking
say	send	tell	want

5 [cassette icon] Read this with a dictionary.

When Jock McHaverty was a little boy, he always wanted to be a bus driver. His father hoped he would go into the family business, and his mother would have liked him to be a doctor. But Jock just wasn't interested. He loved buses – all kinds of buses. He loved the way they looked, the smell of the diesel fuel, and most of all, the wonderful noise they made. When he was fourteen, he went on his first real holiday – a bus trip to the south of England and back. And when he left school two years later, he went straight into the Highland Bus Company.

Now Jock was one of the Company's most experienced drivers, working on the Fort William – Inverness route. This morning was fairly typical: he had eight passengers on board, and would probably pick up one or two more on the way. They were about twenty minutes late (Jock had stopped for a cup of tea and a chat at Strathnahuilish Post Office), but it didn't matter. 'Late' was not a word of any great importance in the Scottish Highlands. Jock leaned forward a little in his seat and smiled. It was a lovely day. The sun was shining on the loch, and the bus was running beautifully. Jock changed gear as they started up the long hill towards Clandonald Castle.

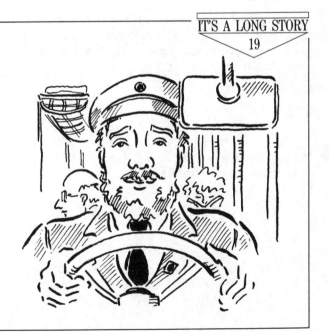

IT'S A LONG STORY
19

THERE IS NO PRACTICE BOOK WORK FOR LESSON 20D.

Unit 21 Knowing about the future

21A I'm going to learn Chinese

1 What are you going to do this evening? Tomorrow? Next weekend? Next year? Write at least eight sentences.

2 Say these sentences with the correct stress.

1. **What** are you **going** to **do**?
2. I'm **not going** to **have** a **hol**iday **this year**.
3. I'm **never** going to **speak** to you a**gain**.
4. **Who's** going to **clean** the **car**?
5. **What film** are you going to **see**?

3 Choose the correct tense.

1. I .... Lucy since Friday. (*haven't seen / didn't see*)
2. My mother .... Mrs Carpenter better than I do. (*knows / has known*)
3. She .... her for years. (*knows / has known*)
4. How long .... English? (*have you been learning / are you learning / do you learn*)
5. I .... John yesterday. (*saw / have seen*)
6. He says he .... round to see us this evening. (*'s coming / comes*)
7. What .... this evening? (*are you doing / do you do*)
8. It usually .... a lot in November. (*is raining / rains*)
9. Mark and Susan .... next month. (*are getting married / get married*)

4 If you have Student's Cassette B, find Unit 21, Lesson A, Exercise 3. Listen and try to write down the conversation. Difficult words: *lucky, afford, spring, summer.*

5 People's plans.
1. Read the first text.
2. Complete the second text with words and expressions from the first text.
3. Write about the plans of somebody you know who is going to study.

SATISH'S PLANS
Satish has just left school. Next year he is going to travel. He says 'I want to get some experience of life before I start studying.' He is going to spend six months in South America and six months in the Far East. First of all he is going to get a job in a factory in Brasilia – his father has got business contacts there. When he goes to the Far East he is going to try to find work teaching English.

After his year abroad Satish in going to study engineering at St Andrews University in Scotland.

RUTH'S PLANS
Ruth .... to leave school next summer. She .... to .... engineering at Brunel University, ... London, but before going there she wants to .... a year working. She says '...............
.... some work experience ....
....' She is .... spend six months in Italy and six .... in Britain, working in car .... where her teacher has got ....

21B This is going to be the kitchen

1 Make sentences with *is/are going to.*

1. What time | you | be | home tonight?
   <u>What time are you going</u>
   <u>to be home tonight ?</u>
2. When | your parents | move to London?
3. Why | your son | study engineering?
4. How | we all | travel to Scotland?
5. Where | Alice | buy her new car?
6. Who | cook supper?

2 Read the problem and see if you can find the answer.

Five children, still at school, are going to be a doctor, an engineer, a teacher, a lorry driver and a tennis player. Kate is not going to study after leaving school. George is going to be either the doctor or the teacher. One of the children is going to have a job which begins with the same letter as his/her name. Mark is not going to be the doctor or the engineer. Louise is not going to be the doctor. What is Phil going to be?

(Solution on page 133.)

3 Stress. Say these words (they are all stressed on the first syllable).

breakfast **num**ber **dic**tionary **bed**room
bathroom **fin**ished **some**where

Now say these (they are all stressed on the second syllable).

in**clud**ing with**out** ex**pen**sive de**pends**
de**cide** re**mem**ber for**get**

Now say these (they are all stressed on the third syllable).

infor**ma**tion conver**sa**tion under**stand**

4 Learn these irregular verbs.

INFINITIVE	PAST TENSE	PAST PARTICIPLE
bring	brought	brought
buy	bought	bought
begin	began	begun
take	took	taken
wear	wore	worn

5 Look at the picture. Do you know the names of all these vehicles?
Look up and learn the ones you don't know.

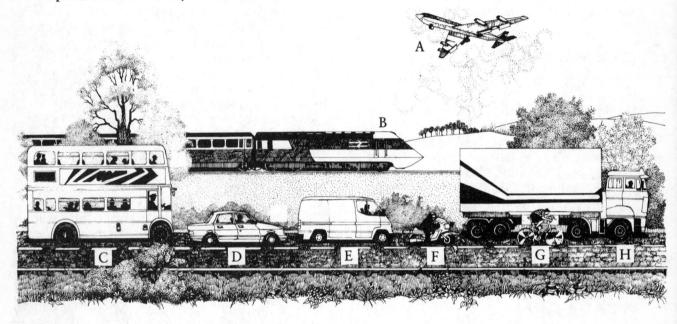

21C It's going to rain

1 Look at each picture and say what is going to happen.

2 What is going to happen in the next hour? Write down as many things as you can think of.

3 Pronunciation. Say these sentences.

Where are you going to **live**?
Who are you **going** to **see**?
When are you going to **pay**?
Why are you going to **do** it?

My **parents** are going to **move** to London.
The **children** are **going** to **leave school**.
Prices are going to **go up**.

4 Do you know the names of the different parts of the body?

21D   Why? To . . .

1 Tourists go to Switzerland to climb the mountains, or to ski, or to enjoy the scenery. They go to the USA to see New York, or to visit the West, or to practise speaking English. Write ten sentences to say why tourists go to France, or to Britain, or to India, or to Japan, or to other countries.

2 Write five or more sentences like these.

People don't go to Nigeria to ski.
People don't go to Iceland to drink wine.

3 Write about some places that you have been to, and your reasons for going. Example:

I went to Madrid last weekend to see

my cousins.

4 Vocabulary revision. Do you know all these words? Can you pronounce them? Check in your dictionary if you're not sure.

plane; tennis; animal; language; kiss; play; watch; listen (to); change; learn; buy; borrow; meet; understand; travel; north; south; east; west; hard; cold; tired; young; interesting; across; because.

5 Translate these into your language.

1. Peter and Ann are going to get married.
2. This is going to be the children's room.
3. The bathroom is going to be on the ground floor.
4. She's going to have a baby.
5. I went to the library to borrow a book.
6. I went to a bookshop to buy a book.
7. People learn English all over the world.
8. I'm learning English to do business in English-speaking countries.

6 📟 Read this with a dictionary.

IT'S A LONG STORY
20

In her black Porsche, Dr Wagner was getting a little impatient. She was in a hurry to get to her hotel in Inverness and have a bath and a rest, after driving overnight from London. But for the last fifteen miles she had been stuck behind a bus that was driving very slowly in the middle of the road, and it seemed impossible to get past. 'Calm down, Mary,' she said to herself. 'You've got plenty of time.'

She started thinking about the holiday that was just starting. Every year, she drove up to the Scottish Highlands and spent two weeks looking for the Loch Ness Monster. Dr Wagner was a member of the West London Society for the Investigation of Strange and Unexplained Phenomena, and she was very interested in monsters, ghosts, flying saucers and things of that kind. She had never yet seen anything in Loch Ness, but she always had a wonderful holiday and went back home feeling happy and relaxed. She had a feeling about this year, though. This year was going to be special. Somehow, she just knew.

A sudden noise brought her out of her dreams. She looked in the mirror. Behind her, the road was full of police cars, with lights flashing and sirens howling. Dr Wagner frowned. She didn't like police cars. 'It's no use making all that noise,' she said. 'You'll never get past the bus.'

"This is a pretty tough library!"

Unit 22 Telling people to do things

22A I feel ill

1 Complete the exchanges.

A: I've got a cold.
B: ....?

A: How are you?
B: .... ill.
A: ....?

A: I've got ....
B: ....?

A: What's the problem?
B: ....

* * *

A: Why don't you go to bed?
B: ....

* * *

A: .... temperature?
B: I don't think so.

2 Write two or three sentences to say how you feel just now.

3 Put one of these words in each blank.

I	you	he	she	it	we	they
me	you	him	her	it	us	them
my	your	his	her	its	our	their

1. My brothers and I all look like .... mother.
2. Tell the children to bring .... favourite toys.
3. Mum's gone to bed – .... says .... is tired.
4. Did you write to Jim or talk to .... on the phone?
5. Could you show .... that ring, please?
6. Don't worry about me and the children – .... will eat along the way somewhere.
7. I really like Don and Susan – .... are so easy to be with.
8. You can borrow .... map if you haven't got one.
9. Tell .... what the problem is and we will try to help you with it.
10. My brother lent me .... car last weekend.

4 If you have Student's Cassette B, find Unit 22, Lesson A, Exercise 2. Listen and repeat. Try for very good stress and intonation.

WOMAN: Good morning, Mr Culham. How are you?
MAN: I feel ill.
WOMAN: I *am* sorry. What's the matter?
MAN: My eyes hurt, and I've got a bad headache.
WOMAN: Oh, I hope you aren't catching flu. Why don't you take an aspirin?
MAN: That's a good idea.

5 The pictures are in order but the text is not. Match the parts of the text to the pictures. You can use your dictionary.

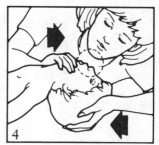
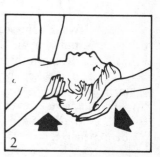

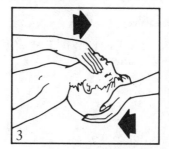
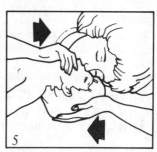

a. Breathe into the child, but not too strongly. (A small child's lungs cannot hold your entire breath.) Take your lips away and let the child's chest go down while you take your next breath. Use fairly quick, short breaths, and keep it up until the child can breathe by himself or until help comes, as long as two hours.

b. Open the air passages by pulling the neck up and putting the head down very far.

c. If the child has got water in his lungs, first get it out by putting him on his stomach for ten seconds with his hips a foot higher than his head (over your knee, on a box, etc.).

d. Keep the child's chin pushed up all the time, to keep the air passages open.

e. With a child's small face you can breathe into nose and mouth together.

(from *Baby and Child Care* by Dr Benjamin Spock – adapted)

22B Always warm up

1 Here are some instructions about how to drive a car. Put *always*, *never* or *don't* before each one. Use a dictionary.

1. .... look in the mirror before driving off.
2. .... drive fast in fog.
3. .... drive too close to the car in front.
4. .... forget to check the oil from time to time.
5. .... wear your seat belt.
6. .... put a small child in the front seat.
7. .... drive on the right in Britain.
8. .... overtake when you can't see a long way in front.
9. .... drive at over 30 miles an hour in towns.
10. .... park on a double yellow line – it can be expensive.

2 Copy and complete the table.

INFINITIVE	PAST TENSE	PAST PARTICIPLE
come	came	come
....	cost	....
....	....	drawn
drink	....	....
....	ate	....
....	....	forgotten
get	....	....
....	gave	....
....	....	gone/been
leave	....	....

3 If you have Student's Cassette B, find Unit 22, Lesson B, Exercise 2 (only part of the boy's answer is recorded here). Listen, and write down everything you can.

4 Read the text and put the pictures in the right order.

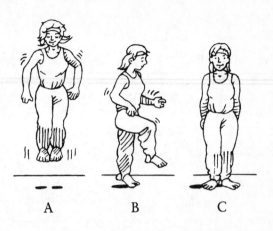

A   B   C

> **Exercise Ten   Run and hop**
>
> **Start** Stand erect, feet together, arms at sides. Starting with left leg, run in place raising feet at least four inches from floor.
> (When running in place lift knees forward, do not merely kick heels backwards.)
>
> **Count** Each time left foot touches floor counts one. After each fifty counts do ten hops.
>
> **Hops** Hopping is done so that both feet leave floor together. Try to hop at least four inches off floor each time.
>
> (from *Physical Fitne*

5 Fast reading. Read these instructions fast but carefully, and do exactly what they say. Time limit: two minutes.

Write your surname on a piece of paper. Don't write your first name. If it is Tuesday, write your age, but if it is Thursday, write the date. If it is not Tuesday or Thursday, don't write anything, but draw a big O round your name. Write the name of your country, in English, under your name. If you have not already written the date, write it to the left of the name of your country. If you are over thirty, do not write the name of an animal, but if you are thirty or under, write the name of an animal and the name of a bird at the bottom of the page.

"Very good, chaps, now we'll try it from the plane."

22C Look out!

1 Put the words with the right notices. Use a dictionary.

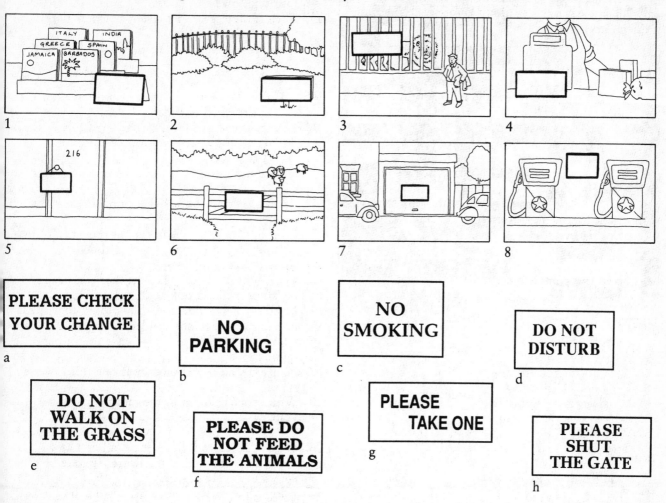

**PLEASE CHECK
YOUR CHANGE**

a

**NO
PARKING**

b

**NO
SMOKING**

c

**DO NOT
DISTURB**

d

**DO NOT
WALK ON
THE GRASS**

e

**PLEASE DO
NOT FEED
THE ANIMALS**

f

**PLEASE
TAKE ONE**

g

**PLEASE
SHUT
THE GATE**

h

2 Write three or more notices for your school.

3 Put one of these expressions in each blank.

> look out   come in   look   don't worry
> wait here   follow me   be careful
> please hurry   take your time

1. _Be careful_ — there are eggs in that box.
2. .... Everything's all right.
3. .... and sit down, Mr Pearson. What can I do for you?
4. .... My plane is at four o'clock, and it's 3.15 now.
5. ...., please. Your seats are right over here.
6. ....! There's your brother over there!
7. ....! There's a car coming!
8. Ms Wilsdon is busy at the moment. Could you ...., please?
9. 'I'm terribly sorry.' 'That's all right. I'm not in a hurry. ....'

4 Copy and complete the table.

INFINITIVE	PAST TENSE	PAST PARTICIPLE
lend	....	....
....	lay	....
....	....	made
....	....	meant
meet	....	....
....	ran	....
....	....	said
send	....	....
....	showed	....
....	....	sung

5 Vocabulary revision. Do you know all these words? Can you pronounce them? Check in your dictionary if you're not sure.

leg; eye; idea; water; road; run; walk; drink; right; better; comfortable; fast; rich; somebody; until; over.

6 If you have Student's Cassette B, find Unit 22, Lesson C, Exercise 2 (only the first part is recorded here). Look up these words in your dictionary: *comfortably*; *cow*; *farm*. Then listen to the cassette, as many times as you want, and try to write down all the words.

7 Try the crossword.

(Solution on page 133.)

ACROSS

1. £ $ DM ¥
6. .... are you from?
8. The opposite of *cheap*.
10. My sister can run faster .... me.
12. Eyes can be this colour.
13. Why don't you go .... and lie down?
14. Opposite of *good*.
18. .... the first left.
19. I can't drink this coffee – it's .... hot.
21. The opposite of *hot*.
22. Husband and ....
23. Mountains are ....
24. He can't walk home; it's .... too far.
25. Me, ..., her, him, us, them.
26. The opposite of *2 down*.
28. Their children are still ....; the oldest is three.

31. Susan is the .... interesting person I know.
32. There's a lot of .... in my study; it has got four windows.
33. Alice is taller than her sister, but they both weigh the same; Alice is ....
34. 'Jane, you look ill!' 'Yes, I feel ill. I think I've got a ....'

DOWN

1. My brother .... a beautiful cake for his girlfriend's birthday.
2. You can't talk in my car – it's too ....
3. I always wear comfortable clothing .... I run.
4. How many people .... there in your English class?
5. I don't like my son to walk home .... at night.
7. Everybody .... Ann caught the early train.
9. A Volkswagen is more .... than a Rolls-Royce.
10. I don't think .... her brother can drive.
11. He's not .... tall .... his wife.
15. My daughter is fair now, but I think that she'll be .... when she's older.
16. I can't phone her .... I haven't got her number.
17. People are in this room about one third of their time.
20. When you wake up in the morning, you .... your eyes.
22. '................?' 'Because.'
26. She's .... tall, but not as tall as I am.
27. How far is it .... the nearest phone box?
29. The same as *32 across*.
30. I don't like opera; rock music is much .... interesting.
31. Yesterday at a party I .... somebody who has got the same birthday as me.

22D   Please speak more slowly

1 Make adverbs from these adjectives.

tired *tiredly*

easy last sensitive possible probable certain careful different quick heavy

2 Put the adverb in the right place.

1. She opened every book. (*carefully*)
2. I like British television. (*very much*)
3. She read the newspaper. (*quickly*)
4. He said 'No' and walked away. (*angrily*; *fast*)
5. He answered the phone. (*sleepily*)
6. Please say your name and age. (*clearly*)

3 Revision. Put in the past tenses of the verbs.

1. I .... your mother yesterday. She's looking fine. (*see*)
2. You .... a letter from Sylvia this morning, didn't you? (*get*)
3. Who .... St Paul's Cathedral? (*build*)
4. I .... ill yesterday, so I .... to see the doctor. (*feel*; *go*)
5. It .... very late when I .... home last night. (*be*; *come*)
6. Alex .... a new car last week. (*buy*)
7. A man once .... 6,700m without a parachute, and lived. (*fall*)
8. My boss .... to New York again last week. (*fly*)

4 Translate these into your language.

1. What's the matter?
2. I feel ill.
3. I've got a cold.
4. I've got toothache.
5. My leg hurts.
6. Don't run if you feel tired.
7. Please hurry, darling.
8. Take your time.
9. Be careful.
10. Look out!
11. Follow me, please.
12. I'm very angry with you.
13. She spoke to me very angrily.
14. You speak English very well.

5 If you have Student's Cassette B, find Unit 22, Lesson D, Exercise 1. Listen and try to write the sentences.

6 Read this letter; you can use a dictionary. Then write a letter telling a friend about your home.

Dear Alice,

I'm so happy I can lend you my flat while you're here: I'm only sorry I can't be here with you.

Mrs Rogers on the first floor has got the keys for you, and she is looking forward to seeing you. She is very friendly, and she will happily tell you about shopping and so on.

Please lock the door carefully when you go out, and when you are in the flat; remember that this is a big city, not like your little village! The milkman will leave you a pint of milk every two days, but if you want to change that just leave him a note. And could you water my plants when they are dry? They will do well if you water them every three days or so, but they will die fast if you give them too much water.

I hope you have a lovely time. I will leave a note in the flat about interesting places to go and interesting things to do.

Love,

Janice

7 📼 Read this with a dictionary.

IT'S A LONG STORY
21

Down at the bottom of Loch Ness, things were very calm. The Monster scratched her ear with the third leg on the right and decided that it was time to do something. She didn't usually go up to the surface during the day because the light hurt her eyes, but she was getting bored out of her mind sitting down at the bottom of the loch with nothing to do except talk to the fish. She scratched her ear again, yawned, stretched, and started swimming slowly up towards the light.

Five minutes later, the Monster reached the surface, stuck her head and fifteen metres of neck out of the water, and looked around. She closed her eyes and opened them again. It was a little difficult to understand what was happening. Scotland was generally a fairly quiet place, but today a lot of things seemed to be going on.

On the bank of the loch, two women were fighting. A man was trying to stop them; another man was trying to learn to swim. The road was full of cars with pretty blue lights on top, coming from all directions. A helicopter landed on the bank of the loch and some soldiers got out and lay down. There was a bus driving along very slowly with the driver looking out of the window. The bus driver caught sight of the Monster and drove into the loch. The two women stopped fighting and stood with their mouths open. All the police cars crashed into each other. A sports car stopped and a woman got out and started taking photographs.

It was all too much. The Monster closed her eyes and went back down to the bottom of the loch.

Unit 23 Predictions

23A Are you sure you'll be all right?

1 What presents do you think people will give you next Christmas, or on your next birthday? Use *I (don't) think, I'm sure, perhaps, probably.*
Examples:

I think my father will give me a book.
Perhaps somebody will give me perfume.
I don't think anybody will give me a car.

2 Read these sentences with the correct stress.

I'm going to **hitch**hike **round** the **world**.
Where will you **sleep**?
You'll **get lost**.
What will you **do** for **money**?
Of **course** I'll be **all right**.

3 Use five or more of these words to write some true sentences about yourself.

didn't	last night	woke	knew	came
went	lived	will	never	happy

4 Copy and complete the table.

INFINITIVE	PAST TENSE	PAST PARTICIPLE
go	went	gone/been
say	....	said
....	took	....
buy	....	....
....	....	spoken
....	left	....
understand	....	....
....	....	given
....	knew	....
write	....	....
....	....	read
....	came	....

5 If you have Student's Cassette B, find Unit 23, Lesson A, Exercise 1. Listen to the conversation and practise the pronunciation.

23B If you push lever B, . . .

1 Choose words to complete these sentences. Try to do the exercise first without looking at the list of words. (There are three extra words in the list.)

1. I was .... in London, ... 16 June 1942, ... three o'clock .... the morning. I was a beautiful ....
2. I had a very strange .... last night. I was in a big red Rolls-Royce. We were going .... York, and we were .... very fast in the dark, without .... Suddenly I .... a white horse in the road .... front .... us. Then I .... up.
3. 'What did she want?' 'I don't know. She .... so quietly that I couldn't .... what she said.'
4. What's that noise in the street? Look .... the window and see what's ....

again	at	baby	born	dream	driving
happening	hear	in	in	lights	long
of	on	out of	saw	shop	spoke
to	woke				

2 Say where you got some of your possessions.
Examples:

I got my sweater in London.
I got my watch from my mother.
I got my shirt at the shop round the corner.

3 Say these sentences with the correct stress.

What are they **doing**?
Where are you **going**?
What do you **think**?
When can I **come**?
How do you **know**?
Who did you **see**?
Why do you **ask**?
What does she **want**?
When did they **arrive**?
How can I **help**?

4 Fast reading. Read the text and find the answers to the questions as fast as you can. Time limit: two minutes.

mph	km/h	Record	mph	km/h	Record
622.287	1001.473	Highest land speed (four wheeled rocket powered) (Official land speed record)	43.14	69.40	Track cycling (219 yd *200 m* unpaced in 10.369 s)
429.311	690.909	Highest land speed (wheel driven)	41.72	67.14	Greyhound racing (410 yd *374 m* straight 26.13 s)
319.627	514.39	Official water speed record	41.50	66.78	Sailing – 60 ft *18,29 m* proa Crossbow II (36.04 kts)
318.866	513.165	Highest speed motor cycle	35.06	56.42	Horse racing – The Derby (1 mile 885 yd *2.41 km*)
250.958	403.878	Motor racing – closed circuit	27.00	43.5	Sprinting (during 100 yd *91 m*)
188	302.5	Pelota	25.78	41.48	Roller skating (400 yd *402 m* in 34.9 s)
170	273	Golf ball	21.49	34.58	Cycling – average maintained over 24 hr
163.6	263	Lawn tennis – serve	13.46	21.67	Rowing (2187 yd *2000 m*)
140.5	226.1	Cycling, motor paced	12.26	19.74	Marathon run (26 miles 385 yd *42.195 km*)
128.16	206.25	Water skiing	9.39	15.121	Walking – 1 hr
124.412	200.222	Downhill Schuss (alpine skiing)	5.28	8.50	Swimming (50 yd) – short course in 19.36 s
63.894	102.828	Downhill alpine skiing (Olympic course) (average)	4.53	7.29	Swimming (*100 m*) – long course in 49.36 s
52.57	84.60	Speedway (4 laps of 430 yd *393 m*)			
43.26	69.62	Horse racing (440 yd *402 m* in 20.8 s)			

SPEED IN SPORT

(from *Guinness Book of Answers* – abridged)

1. What is the record speed for a tennis serve?
2. What is the record average speed for 24-hour cycling?
3. What is the official land speed record?
4. What is the water skiing record speed?
5. What is the record speed for a one-hour walk?

23C What do the stars say?

1 Put in the correct form (Future with *will* or Simple Past).

1. My horoscope said 'You _will have_ a wonderful week' (*have*)
2. but actually, I .... a terrible week. (*have*)
3. My horoscope said 'You .... on a long journey' (*go*)
4. but actually, I only .... to the post office. (*go*)
5. My horoscope said 'Money .... to you' (*come*)
6. but actually, I .... the whole week paying bills. (*spend*)
7. My horoscope said 'You .... a tall dark stranger' (*meet*)
8. but actually, I .... a short fat policeman. (*meet*)
9. My horoscope said 'This .... a good time for love' (*be*)
10. but actually, my girlfriend .... very unkind to me. (*be*)
11. My horoscope said 'There .... bad news on Wednesday'. (*be*)
12. Actually, there .... bad news every day. (*be*)

2 Choose three or more of these lists and see how many words you can add.

1. red, blue, . . .
2. coat, sweater, . . .
3. table, chair, . . .
4. orange, fish, . . .
5. secretary, shop assistant, . . .
6. happy, tired, . . .
7. shy, bad-tempered, . . .
8. post office, station, . . .

3 Learn these irregular verbs.

INFINITIVE	PAST TENSE	PAST PARTICIPLE
sit	sat	sat
sleep	slept	slept
speak	spoke	spoken
spend	spent	spent
stand	stood	stood
swim	swam	swum
tell	told	told
think	thought	thought
understand	understood	understood
wake	woke	woken

4 Translate one of the horoscopes from Student's Book page 114 into your language.

5 Imagine a 'dream holiday' for yourself next year. What will happen? Where will you go? Who will you meet? What will you do?

→

6 Read this with a dictionary.

(*Which?* is the magazine of the Consumers' Association. It tests different things that you can buy, and says which is the 'best buy'. One month, *Which?* tested horoscopes.)

Most people will say there's nothing in horoscopes. So you would expect that most people wouldn't read them. But they do.

We thought we would try to find out how useful forecasts from stars really are, in their most accessible form – horoscopes in the press.

First of all we asked 1,000 people whether they read horoscopes, whether they found them useful, and what their reactions were.

Their reactions ranged from 'nonsense' and 'a load of rubbish' through 'they're fun' and 'amusing', to one person who always looked at them 'before making any major decision'.

To find out how good the advice and predictions really are, and see if there was any best buy, we asked some 200 people, some men, some women, some believers and some not, to read their horoscopes in the papers and magazines every day for a month, and to comment on them at the end of each day.

Rather sadly, 83 per cent reported that the advice was very little help at all. There wasn't much to choose between any of the newspapers and magazines we looked at but *Woman*, *Woman's Own* and the *Daily Mirror* were thought marginally less unhelpful than the average, while the *Sun* and the *News of the World* were thought worse.

"*Separate futures, please.*"

"*I've already met the tall, dark man. What I'd like to know is, where is he now?*"

23D What will happen next?

1 What will fashions be like 50 years from now?
Complete some or all of these sentences.

I think skirts will be _longer._
I think the fashionable colour will be . . .
I'm sure people will wear . . .
I'm sure people won't wear . . .
I don't think people will wear . . .
People certainly won't wear . . .
Perhaps men will wear . . .
Perhaps women will wear . . .
Clothes will be . . .

2 Pronounce these words (they all have the same vowel sound).

first   heard   word   early   certain
Thursday   work   shirt   skirt   turn
third   learn   sir   dirty   girl

3 Prepositions. Complete the sentences.

1. Our house is right .... the police station.
2. I heard a strange noise .... the night.
3. Don't run until two hours .... eating.
4. We're very old friends. We met ....
   university.
5. I've been here .... six weeks, and I still can't
   understand anybody.
6. Would you like a drink .... you go to bed?
7. I'll meet you at the station, ... the clock.
8. The bus arrives .... the airport ....
   about 10.25.
9. Come and sit .... me. I want to tell you
   something.
10. Are you doing anything .... Tuesday?

4 Vocabulary revision. Do you know all these
words and expressions? Can you pronounce them?
Check in a dictionary if you're not sure.

money; driver; help; party; parents; street; sleep;
need; get up; hope; open; agree; sure; hard;
interesting; strange; rich; terrible; early; late; again;
enough; round the world.

5 Translate these into your language.

1. I'm going to be a racing driver.
2. That's very dangerous.
3. I don't mind.
4. You'll get killed.
5. No, I won't.
6. My English is getting better.
7. What time do you usually get up?
8. Get on the bus outside the station, and get off at
   the post office.

6 🔊 Read this with a dictionary.

IT'S A LONG STORY
22

'Hello, Judy,' said Dr Wagner. 'What are you doing here? I
thought you were in Rio.' 'It's a long story,' said Judy. 'I'll
tell you later.' 'Did you see the Monster?' said Dr Wagner.
'Wasn't she just *wonderful*? I got hundreds of photos.'

'I'm sorry to interrupt,' said Jasper, 'but I think this is a
very good time to go on holiday. Isabel, go and get Sam
out of the water and follow us up to the castle. Judy, come
with me. I hope the ghost remembered to fill the plane up
with petrol.' 'Ghost?' said Dr Wagner. 'You have a ghost in
your castle? *A ghost?*' 'Come along with us and you can
meet him,' said Judy. 'But hurry.'

Twenty seconds later, they drove in through the front
gate of the castle in Dr Wagner's Porsche, and a minute or
so after that Isabel ran up carrying Sam over her shoulder.
The ghost closed the gate and led the way to the back of
the castle. There, standing on the grass, shining in the
sun, was a powerful-looking six-seater aeroplane. 'Get in,'
said Jasper. 'We haven't got a moment to lose.' 'Can I
come too?' asked Dr Wagner. 'I must talk to that beautiful
ghost.' 'Of course,' said Jasper, 'but get in fast, or you'll be
talking to our wonderful police. Fasten seat-belts,
everybody. Take-off in fifteen seconds.' 'Where are we
going?' asked Judy. 'Rio,' said Jasper. 'That's where you
wanted to go, isn't it?' 'Sounds good to me,' said Sam.
'Jasper,' said Judy, 'I have been a blind, blind fool. I love
you.'

Unit 24 Consolidation

24A Things to remember: Units 21, 22 and 23

1 Write the adverbs.

angry *angrily*   economical   sure
hungry   noisy   real
beautiful   quiet   comfortable
free   warm

2 Put the adverbs in the right place.

1. She speaks Chinese. (*very well*)
2. Please write your address. (*clearly*)
3. He wrote my name without looking at me. (*slowly*)
4. He closed the door. (*angrily*)
5. Please read this paper. (*carefully*)

3 Complete these sentences.

1. If you ....*don't eat*...., you'll get thin.
2. If you . . . , you'll get tired.
3. If you . . . , you'll get thirsty.
4. If you . . . , you'll get wet.

5. If I . . . , I'll be very happy.
6. If . . . , I'll be very unhappy.
7. If . . . , it will be very bad for the country.
8. If . . . , it will be very good for the country.

4 Read the text, but do not use a dictionary. Then look at the words and expressions, and choose the best explanation for each. After you have done that, check in a dictionary.

'The best car in the world'

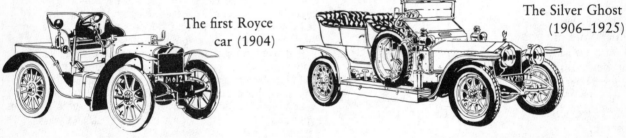

The first Royce car (1904)

The Silver Ghost (1906–1925)

The Silver Cloud (1959–1966)

The Silver Spirit (1981)

Henry Royce did not like his Decauville car, which ran badly and often broke down. So he decided to make a better car himself, and in 1904 he produced his first two-cylinder model. Charles Rolls, a car manufacturer, was very impressed by Royce's car, and soon Rolls and Royce went into business together. One of their first models was the Silver Ghost. In 1907, a Silver Ghost broke the world's endurance record by driving 14,371 miles (23,120km) without breaking down once. After the drive, it cost just over £2 to put the car back into perfect condition. It is not surprising that the Silver Ghost was called 'the best car in the world'. Rolls-Royce cars are famous for running quietly: an advertisement for one model said 'the loudest noise is the ticking of the clock'. The cars are made very carefully. A lot of the work is done by hand, and they take a long time to manufacture: only twelve cars leave the factory every day.

1. *It broke down:* (a) It made a noise. (b) Pieces fell off it. (c) It stopped working.
2. *Charles Rolls was very impressed by Royce's car:* (a) He thought it was good. (b) He wanted it. (c) He did not understand it.
3. *model:* (a) picture (b) small car (c) sort of car
4. *endurance:* (a) going fast (b) going on for a long time (c) being easy to drive
5. *Rolls-Royce cars are famous:* (a) They are very good. (b) Everybody knows about them. (c) They are very quiet.
6. *ticking:* (a) a sort of clock (b) a part of a car (c) a sort of noise
7. *manufacture:* (a) make (b) sell (c) finish
8. *factory:* (a) town (b) place where cars are made (c) shop

5 Try the crossword.

1. Get off the bus .... Park Street.
3. The USA is in .... America.
7. 'I like her.' '................ do I.'
8. Get .... the bus outside the station.
9. I'll phone you again .... three days.

11. You'll get thin if you don't .... enough.
13. Cold time of the year.
15. You can .... a dictionary if you like.
17. Let's meet .... eight o'clock.
18. Warm time of the year.
19. Past of *meet*.
22. After *13 across* and before *18 across*.
24. If you don't eat at all, you'll ....
25. I'm tired – let's .... home.
27. Are you doing anything .... Tuesday?
28. Argentina is in .... America.

D
O
W
N

1. I'm not .... tall as my father.
2. I'm going to the bank .... get some money out.
3. I'm sorry – there's .... more steak.

4. I write to my mother .... a week.
5. My eyes are .... same colour as my mother's.
6. This word comes in two other places in the crossword.
9. *It is* = ...
10. My sister's .... architect.
12. After *18 across* and before *13 across*.
13. The sun is here in the evening.
14. Can you tell me the .... of trains to Exeter?
16. The sun is here in the morning.
20. Food that comes from a bird.
21. Infinitive of *won*.
23. Capitalist without capital.
24. 'How .... you .... ?' 'How .... you .... ?'
26. This is the end .... the crossword.

(Solution on page 133.)

24B Choose

1 You don't know these words. How do you pronounce them? (Don't use a dictionary.)

tope   dune   slot   cope
dram   glide   slid   pride
hack   cube   grid   grate

2 Say these words with the correct stress.

morning   **as**pirin (/ˈæsprɪn/)
medicine (/ˈmedsən/)
headache   **prob**lem   **ter**rible
under**stand**   pro**nounce**
re**mem**ber   for**get**   in**vite**
pre**fer**   in**clud**ed   ex**am**ine
pre**scrip**tion   to**mor**row

3 Put the past form of one of these verbs in each sentence.

begin	buy	can	come	go	have	hear	know
put	say	see	take	tell	wake up		

1. When I .... this morning I was still very tired.
2. I .... Janet at the disco last night.
3. John .... Michael Jackson when he was a boy.
4. I .... some grape juice for you when I went shopping.
5. We .... the children to the Science Museum last week.
6. 'Where's my jacket?' 'I think you .... it on the bed.'
7. He .... he .... a headache, but I think he just didn't want to come.
8. The postman .... very early this morning.
9. When she was younger she .... run much faster than now.
10. They .... to Bali for two weeks in September.
11. Who .... you that I was unhappy?
12. I .... studying English when I was twelve.
13. I was just going to bed when I .... a terrible noise in the street.

4 Vocabulary revision. Do you know all these words? Can you pronounce them? Check in a dictionary if you're not sure.

buy; dog; fall; horse; next; o'clock; pull; sing; turn; word.

5 Use the words and expressions in the box to complete the text. You can use words more than once.

because	but	finally	first of all	how	I'm afraid	so
then	what	when	who			

Yesterday was not a good day. ....1...., I woke up late ....2.... I didn't hear my alarm clock. ....3.... I got out of bed I put my foot on a teacup that was standing by the bed. I can't think ....4.... it got there – perhaps somebody ....5.... doesn't like me put it there while I was asleep. ....6.... I cleaned the tea off the carpet and got dressed as quickly as I could. There wasn't much time, ...7.... I was going to Chester for a job interview, and my train was at seven-forty, and it was already seven twenty-five. ....8.... I couldn't find my keys to open the door. I looked everywhere. ....9.... I decided there was only one thing to do. I opened a window and started climbing out. This was not difficult, ...10.... my flat is on the ground floor, and I am still quite young and athletic – I play tennis every Saturday afternoon, and I do a lot of swimming on holiday. But just as I stood up and closed the window somebody said 'Excuse me, sir.' I turned round and saw that it was a policeman. It was now seven-thirty, ...11.... I didn't really have time for conversation. 'Good morning, officer,' I said. 'I'd like to talk to you, ...12.... I'm afraid I can't stop, ...13.... I've got a train to catch.' 'I'm sure you have, sir,' he said. 'But ....14.... I'll have to ask you a few questions first.' ....15.... I spent an hour and a half at the police station, and I missed the train, and ....16.... I finally got to Chester they said I was too late for the interview. The next train home was at six in the evening, ...17.... I had to spend the day in Chester. It rained all day. Do you want to know ....18.... there is to do in Chester on a wet Thursday afternoon? Don't ask.

6 Write about a bad day that you have had.

24C When you grow up

1 Compare yourself and your life now and ten years ago. Write at least five sentences.
Examples:

Ten years ago I lived in a flat; now I live in a house.
Ten years ago I weighed 55 kilos, and I still do.
I can run faster than I could ten years ago.

2 Put in capital letters and correct punctuation where necessary. Then turn to page 107 and check your answer.

hello judy said dr wagner what are you doing here i thought you were in rio its a long story said judy ill tell you later did you see the monster said dr wagner wasnt she just wonderful i got hundreds of photos

3 Vocabulary. Think of five important words that you don't know in English. Find them in your dictionary and learn them.

4 If you have Student's Cassette B, find Unit 24, Lesson C, Exercise 3 (only the second poem is recorded here). Listen to the poem and try to say it yourself. The text is on page 121 of the Student's Book.

5 🔘 Read this with a dictionary.

IT'S A LONG STORY
23

As the plane flew peacefully south-west across the Atlantic, Judy put her head on Jasper's shoulder and closed her eyes. 'I'm so glad I'm in love with you instead of Sam,' she said. 'It's much nicer. I'm sure we're going to be very happy together. Do you think the others will be all right?' 'I think so,' said Jasper, and kissed her.

Judy listened to the fragments of conversation that came from the seats behind. 'Isabel, you are my favourite detective. Will you teach me to swim?' 'Have some more champagne, ghost.' 'Yes, please. Call me MacDonald.' 'You've got beautiful eyes, Sam.' 'Can ghosts get married?'

'Sounds all right,' said Judy. 'Tell me, are you really terribly rich? How did you get your money? What do you do, actually? How did you get to know Sam? Why did you really hijack that plane?'

'I'll tell you later,' said Jasper. 'It's a long story.'

THERE IS NO PRACTICE BOOK WORK FOR LESSON 24D.

Mini-grammar

112

Special verbs: *be*, *have* (*got*) and *can*

Be

Present tense		
I am (I'm)	am I?	I am (I'm) not
you are (you're)	are you?	you are not (aren't)
he is (he's)	is he?	he is not (isn't)
she is (she's)	is she?	she is not (isn't)
it is (it's)	is it?	it is not (isn't)
we are (we're)	are we?	we are not (aren't)
you are (you're)	are you?	you are not (aren't)
they are (they're)	are they?	they are not (aren't)

I'm sixteen. (~~I have sixteen.~~)
'Are you English?' 'Yes, I am.' ('~~Yes, I'm.~~')
Her name's Ann.
'Is Susan an engineer?' 'Yes, she is.' ('~~Yes, she's.~~')
Are John and his father doctors?
  (~~Are doctors John and his father?~~)
'You're Canadian, aren't you?' 'Yes, that's right.'

Past tense		
I was	was I?	I was not (wasn't)
you were	were you?	you were not (weren't)
he/she/it was	was she *etc.*?	he *etc.* was not (wasn't)
we were	were we?	we were not (weren't)
you were	were you?	you were not (weren't)
they were	were they?	they were not (weren't)

'When you **were** a small child, **were** you happy?'
'Yes, I **was**.' 'No, I **wasn't**.' 'I **was** quite happy.'
Were your parents poor? (~~Were poor your parents?~~)
We **weren't** poor, but we **weren't** rich.
Life **wasn't** hard, but white people **were not** always kind to me.

Pronunciation and rhythm

I was (/wəz/) hungry. Yes, I was (/wɒz/).
I wasn't (/wɒznt/) happy. No, I wasn't (/wɒznt/).
We were (/wə/) poor. Yes, we were (/wɜ:/).
We weren't (/wɜ:nt/) happy. No, we weren't (/wɜ:nt/).

Present Perfect and Future

I **have been** ill for the last few weeks.
Where **has** John **been** all day?

Tomorrow **will be** cold and wet.
I'll **be** back home about six o'clock.

There is

there is (there's)	is there?	there is not (isn't)
there are (–)	are there?	there are not (aren't)
there was	was there?	there was not (wasn't)
there were	were there?	there were not (weren't)

Rhythm and stress

There's a **big table** in my **kitchen**. (/ðəz ə/)
Is there any **milk** in the **fridge**? (/ɪz ðər 'eni/)
Yes, there **is**. (/ðər 'ɪz/)
No, there **isn't**. (/ðər 'ɪznt/)
There **isn't** a **garage**. (/ðər 'ɪznt/)
There was some **coffee** on the **table**. (/ðə wəz səm/)
There **wasn't** any **ice** in her **glass**. (/ðə 'wɒznt/)
There are **two chairs** in the **hall**. (/ðər ə/)
There are some **apples here**. (/ðər ə səm/)
Are there any **oranges**? (/'ɑ: ðər 'eni/)
Yes, there **are**. (/ðər 'ɑ:/)
No, there **aren't**. (/ðər 'ɑ:nt/)
Yes, there's **one**. (/ðəz 'wʌn/)
There **aren't** enough **eggs**. (/ðər 'ɑ:nt/)
There **weren't** any **potatoes**. (/ðə 'wɜ:nt/)

Have (got)

Have got (possession, relationships, etc.)

Present tense		
I have (I've) got you have (you've) got he *etc.* has got (he's got) we have (we've) got you have (you've) got they have (they've) got	have I got? have you got? has she *etc.* got? have we got? have you got? have they got?	I have not (haven't) got you have not (haven't) got he *etc.* has not (hasn't) got we have not (haven't) got you have not (haven't) got they have not (haven't) got

You've **got** beautiful eyes.
'**Have** you **got** any sisters or brothers?'
'Yes, I **have**. I've **got** two sisters.'   'No, I **haven't**.'
'**Has** your mother **got** any sisters?'
   ('Has got your mother any sisters?')
'Yes, she **has**. She's **got** two.'   'No, she **hasn't**.'
We've **got** a new car.
I **haven't got** any money.

1. *Have got* means the same as *have*; we use them both to talk about possession and relationships. British people prefer *have got* when they speak and write informally. Americans more often use *have* without *got*.
2. With *had*, we do not use *got* so often. We often use *did* to make past questions and negatives (see below).
3. *Have* can also mean *eat*, *take*, etc. (see below). With these meanings, we do not use *got*, and we use *do* to make questions and negatives.
4. We also use *have* to make the Perfect tenses of other verbs (see below). We do not use *got* or *do* in this case.

Have (= eat, take, etc.)

Present tense		
I have you have he/she/it has we have you have they have	do I have? do you have? does he/she/it have? do we have? do you have? do they have?	I do not (don't) have you do not (don't) have he/she/it does not (doesn't) have we do not (don't) have you do not (don't) have they do not (don't) have

What time **do** you **have** breakfast?
She always **has** a bath in the morning.
Have a good holiday.

The past of *have got* and *have*

I had you had he/she/it had we had you had they had	did I have? did you have? did he/she/it have? did we have? did you have? did they have?	I did not (didn't) have you did not (didn't) have he/she/it did not (didn't) have we did not (didn't) have you did not (didn't) have they did not (didn't) have

When she was young she **had** long fair hair.
We **didn't have** a car when I was a child.
We **had** a wonderful holiday last summer.
What time **did** you **have** breakfast this morning?

Present Perfect and Future

I **have had** a lot of problems this year.
How long **have** you **had** that car?

I think I'll **have** a bath now.
I don't know if we **will have** time to see your mother.

114

Have and be

When Lucy is hungry she **has** bread and cheese.
When I'm thirsty I **have** a glass of orange juice.
 (~~When I have thirsty . . . I've a glass . . .~~)

When I'm dirty I **have** a bath / a shower.
What colour **is** your car?
What size **are** your shoes?

Can

Present tense
I/you/he/she/it/we/they can (~~he/she/it cans~~) can I/you/*etc*.? (~~do I can?~~) I/you/*etc*. cannot (can't)

I can sing. (~~I can to sing.~~)
I **can't** dance.
'**Can** you swim?' 'Yes, I **can**.'
'**Can** you cook?' 'No, I **can't**.'
Diego **can** dance, but Alice **can't**.
Sorry. I **can't** see you tomorrow.

Pronunciation, rhythm and stress

I can (/kən/) swim, but I can't (/kɑ:nt/) dance.
Yes, I can (/kæn/).

Past and conditional
I/you/*etc*. could could I/you/*etc*.? I/you/*etc*. could not (couldn't)

I **could** swim very well when I was younger.
Could I speak to Alice? (~~Could I to speak . . .~~)
Could you speak more slowly, please?
Could you lend me some bread?

Ordinary verbs: present tenses

Simple Present

I play	do I play?	I do not (don't) play
you play	do you play?	you do not (don't) play
he/she/it plays	does he *etc*. play?	she *etc*. does not (doesn't) play
we play	do we play?	we do not (don't) play
you play	do you play?	you do not (don't) play
they play	do they play?	they do not (don't) play

'I live in Curzon Street.' 'Oh? I do, too.'
'Do you like orange juice?' 'Yes, I do. (~~Yes, I like.~~)
'What time does Karen get up?' 'Half past seven.'
'Does she go to work by car?' 'Yes, she does.' 'No, she doesn't.'
'Do Sam and Virginia live near you?' 'No, they don't.'

Stress

Do you (/dju/) **like** orange **juice**?
Yes, I **do**. No, I **don't**.
What time does (/dəz/) **Karen** get **up**?
Does (/dəz, dʌz/) she **have breakfast**?
Yes, she **does** (/dʌz/). No, she **doesn't** (/'dʌznt/).

Pronunciation of *he/she/it* forms

1. /z/ after vowels and most voiced sounds (/b/, /d/, /g/,
 /v/, /ð/, /l/, /m/, /n/, /ŋ/)

   goes /gəʊz/ sees /si:z/ stands /stændz/ lives /lɪvz/
   tells /telz/ runs /rʌnz/

2. /s/ after most unvoiced sounds (/p/, /t/, /k/, /f/, /θ/)

   stops /stɒps/ starts /stɑ:ts/ looks /lʊks/

3. /ɪz/ after /s/, /z/, /ʃ/, /ʒ/, /tʃ/, /dʒ/

   presses /'presɪz/ uses /'ju:zɪz/ pushes /'pʊʃɪz/
   watches /'wɒtʃɪz/

Spelling of *he/she/it* forms

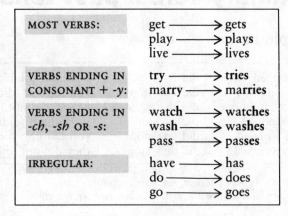

MOST VERBS:	get ⟶ gets play ⟶ plays live ⟶ lives
VERBS ENDING IN CONSONANT + -*y*:	try ⟶ tries marry ⟶ marries
VERBS ENDING IN -*ch*, -*sh* OR -*s*:	watch ⟶ watches wash ⟶ washes pass ⟶ passes
IRREGULAR:	have ⟶ has do ⟶ does go ⟶ goes

Present Progressive

I am ('m) eating	am I eating?	I am ('m) not eating
you are ('re) eating	are you eating?	you are not (aren't) eating
he/she/it is ('s) eating	is he *etc.* eating?	she *etc.* is not (isn't) eating
we are ('re) eating	are we eating?	we are not (aren't) eating
you are ('re) eating	are you eating?	you are not (aren't) eating
they are ('re) eating	are they eating?	they are not (aren't) eating

I'm **looking** for a blue sweater.
Some people **are dancing**.
What **is** the woman in the red dress **doing**?
  (~~What is doing the woman . . .~~)
'**Are** George and Tom **wearing** their blue jackets?'
'Yes, they **are**.'   'No, they **aren't**.'
I'm **not** working today.

Spelling of *-ing* forms

MOST VERBS:	sing ——→ singing
	eat ——→ eating
VERBS ENDING IN *-e*:	make —→ making (~~makeing~~)
	write —→ writing
SHORT VERBS ENDING IN ONE VOWEL + ONE CONSONANT:	stop ——→ stopping
	sit ——→ sitting
	run ——→ running
VERBS ENDING IN *-ie*:	lie ——→ lying

The difference between the two present tenses

1. We use the Simple Present to talk about:

– things that are true all the time

The earth **goes** round the sun.
Water **boils** at 100° Celsius.
I **understand** French.

– things that happen often, usually, sometimes, etc.

I usually **study** from five to seven o'clock.
Helen often **wears** red.

2. We use the Present Progressive to talk about:

– things that are happening now, these days

The water's **boiling**. I'll make coffee.
I'm **studying** very hard just now.
Look. Helen's **wearing** a lovely red dress.

– plans for the future (see below, page 118)

We're **going** to Ann and Peter's for Christmas.
What **are** you **doing** tomorrow?

Telling stories with present tenses

One day, Anna **is walking** in the Tuileries when a man **stops** her. It **is** Boris. He **tells** her . . .

Ordinary verbs: past tenses

Simple Past

I stopped	did I stop?	I did not (didn't) stop
you stopped	did you stop?	you did not (didn't) stop
he/she/it stopped	did she *etc.* stop?	he *etc.* did not (didn't) stop
we stopped	did we stop?	we did not (didn't) stop
you stopped	did you stop?	you did not (didn't) stop
they stopped	did they stop?	they did not (didn't) stop

When Angela was younger, she **hated** school.
'**Did** your family **have** a television when you were a child?'
'No, we **didn't**.'
'**Did** you **like** school when you were a child?'
'Yes, I **did**.' ('~~Yes, I liked.~~')
I **didn't like** cheese when I was a small child, but I do now.
  (~~I liked not cheese . . .   I not liked cheese . . .   I didn't liked cheese . . .~~)

Spelling of regular past tenses

MOST REGULAR VERBS:	work ⟶ worked start ⟶ started wait ⟶ waited play ⟶ played
VERBS ENDING IN -e:	hate ⟶ hated like ⟶ liked
SHORT VERBS ENDING IN ONE VOWEL + ONE CONSONANT:	stop ⟶ stopped shop ⟶ shopped fit ⟶ fitted
VERBS ENDING IN CONSONANT + -y:	study ⟶ studied hurry ⟶ hurried

Pronunciation of regular past tenses

1. /d/ after vowels and voiced sounds (/b/, /g/, /v/, /ð/, /l/, /z/, /ʒ/, /dʒ/, /m/, /n/, /ŋ/)

   agreed /ə'griːd/ played /pleɪd/ lived /lɪvd/ pulled /pʊld/ used /juːzd/

2. /t/ after /p/, /k/, /f/, /θ/, /s/, /ʃ/, /tʃ/

   stopped /stɒpt/ worked /wɜːkt/ watched /wɒtʃt/

3. /ɪd/ after /t/ and /d/

   started /'stɑːtɪd/ decided /dɪ'saɪdɪd/

Present Perfect

(have + past participle)		
I have ('ve) seen you have ('ve) seen he/she/it has ('s) seen we have ('ve) seen you have ('ve) seen they have ('ve) seen	have I seen? have you seen? has he etc. seen? have we seen? have you seen? have they seen?	I have not (haven't) seen you have not (haven't) seen she etc. has not (hasn't) seen we have not (haven't) seen you have not (haven't) seen they have not (haven't) seen

'**Have** you ever **been** to Africa?' 'Yes, I have.'
'**Have** you **seen** *Carmen* before?' 'No, I haven't.'
I've never **learnt** to drive.
I've **changed** my job three times this year.
How long **have** you **lived** in this town?
    (How long do you live in this town?)
How long **have** you **known** Maria?
    (How long do you know Maria?)
I've **known** her since 1986. (I know her since 1986.)
I've **been** in this class for three weeks.
    (I am in this class for three weeks.)
    (I've been in this class since three weeks.)
How long **have** you **been** learning English?

Since and *for*

since + beginning of period = *for* + period

since yesterday = **for** 24 hours
since the 16th century = **for** 400 years

The difference between the Simple Past and the Present Perfect

1. We use the Present Perfect:
   – when we are thinking of a period of time that is not finished (for example *this week/month/year, since . . .*)
   – when we mean 'at any time up to now' (for example, with *ever, never, before*)

   I've **changed** my job three times **this year**.
   Have you **seen** *Carmen* **before**?
   Have you **ever been** to America?
   She **has never learnt** to drive.

2. We use the Simple Past:
   – when we are thinking of a period of time that is finished (for example with *ago, yesterday, last week/month/year* etc., *then, when*)

   I **changed** my job **last week**.
   I **saw** *Carmen* three years **ago**.
     (. . . ago three years . . . before three years)
   Did you **go** to California **last summer**?
   She **learnt** to fly **when** she was eighteen.

The difference between the Present Perfect and the Present

To say *how long* something has been happening, use a Present Perfect tense, not a Present tense. Compare:

I **know** her well.
I **have known** her **since** 1980. (I know her since 1980.)

We **live** in Harwich.
We **have lived** here **for** ten years. (We live here for 10 years.)

She **is** in the advanced class.
She's **been** in the class **for** three weeks. (She is . . .)

Infinitive, past tense and past participle

INFINITIVE	PAST TENSE	PAST PARTICIPLE
Regular verbs		
work	worked	worked
play	played	played
live	lived	lived
stop	stopped	stopped
try	tried	tried
etc.		
Irregular verbs		
be	was/were	been
come	came	come
go	went	been/gone
know	knew	known
learn	learnt	learnt
see	saw	seen

(For a complete list of irregular verbs in *The New Cambridge English Course* Level 1, see Student's Book page 136.)

Talking about the future

Present Progressive (plans)

Are you **doing** anything this evening?
I'm **working** on Thursday.
We're **leaving** on Monday.
We're **travelling** round Australia for three months.
Jane's granny **is** probably **coming** on Thursday.

Be going + infinitive (plans and predictions)

Plans
I'm **going to learn** Chinese.
What **are** you **going to do** next year?
This **is going to be** the kitchen.

Predictions
It's **going to rain**.
The plane's **going to crash**.
She's **going to have** a baby.

Will (predictions)

I/you/he/*etc*. will ('ll) go (~~I will to go~~   ~~he wills go~~)
will I/*etc*. go? (~~do I will go?~~)
I/*etc*. will not (won't) go

I think Manchester **will beat** Liverpool 2–0.
Something very strange **will happen** next Thursday.
Tomorrow **will be** warm and sunny.
If you don't eat you'**ll die**.
Are you sure you'**ll be** all right?

There will be and *it will be*

There will be + noun

There will be **snow**.
There will be **a meeting** at eight o'clock this evening.

It will be + adjective

It will be **cold**.
It won't be very **interesting**.

Present Progressive, *going to* and *will*: the differences

1. Plans:
   We use both the Present Progressive and *going to* to talk about plans. We use the Present Progressive especially when we talk about times and places.
   Compare:

   I'm **going to travel** round the world.
   I'm **travelling** to France next week.

2. Predictions:
   We use both *going to* and *will* to predict (to say what we think or know will happen in the future). We prefer *going to* when we can 'see things coming' – when it is very clear what is going to happen.
   Compare:

   Look! It's **going to rain**.
   Perhaps it **will snow** tomorrow.

   She's **going to have** a baby.
   Do you think the baby **will have** blue eyes?

Imperatives, infinitives and *-ing* forms

Imperatives

Examples: *run; tell; don't run; don't tell*

We use imperatives for giving advice and instructions.

Run early in the morning – it's better.
Meet me at seven o'clock.
Always wear comfortable clothing.
　(~~Wear always comfortable clothing.~~)
Never run in fog. (~~Run never in fog.~~)

Don't run if you've got a cold.
Don't tell Carola.

Infinitives with *to*

Examples: *to see; to go*

We use infinitives with *to*:

– after certain verbs (for example *hope, want, have, would like*)

I **hope to see** you soon.
I **don't want to go** home.
You **have to change** at Coventry.
Would you **like to dance**?

– after *something, anything, nothing*

Would you like **something to eat**?
Have you got **anything to drink**?
There's **nothing to do**.

– to say why we do things ('infinitive of purpose')

'Why did you come here?'　'**To see** you.' (~~For see you.~~)
You go to a supermarket **to buy** food.

Infinitives without *to*

Examples: *see; go*

We use infinitives without *to*:

– after the special verbs *can, could, will, would* and *do*

I **can speak** German.
Could you **speak** more slowly?
It **will rain** tomorrow.
What **would** you **like**?
Does he **smoke**?
Don't stop.

– after *Let's*

Let's all **go** and **see** Ann.

-ing forms

Examples: *seeing; going*

We use *-ing* forms:

– after certain verbs (for example *like, love, hate*)

I **like speaking** French.
I **love going** to the theatre.

– in progressive tenses

'What are you **doing**?'　'I'm **writing** letters.'

– after all prepositions

Thank you **for coming**.
She's good **at swimming**.

Nouns and articles

Plurals of nouns

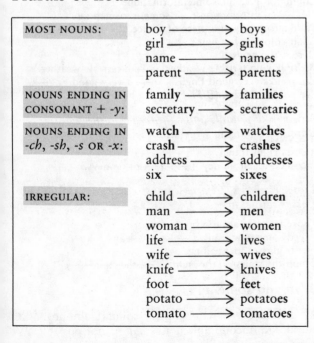

MOST NOUNS:	boy → boys
	girl → girls
	name → names
	parent → parents
NOUNS ENDING IN CONSONANT + -y:	family → families
	secretary → secretaries
NOUNS ENDING IN -ch, -sh, -s OR -x:	watch → watches
	crash → crashes
	address → addresses
	six → sixes
IRREGULAR:	child → children
	man → men
	woman → women
	life → lives
	wife → wives
	knife → knives
	foot → feet
	potato → potatoes
	tomato → tomatoes

Pronunciation of plural *-s*

1. /z/ after vowels and most voiced sounds (/b/, /d/, /g/, /v/, /ð/, /l/, /m/, /n/, /ŋ/)

   days /deɪz/　trees /triːz/　heads /hedz/
   wives /waɪvz/　miles /maɪlz/　pens /penz/

2. /s/ after most unvoiced sounds (/p/, /t/, /k/, /f/, /θ/)

   cups /kʌps/　plates /pleɪts/　books /bʊks/

3. /ɪz/ after /s/, /z/, /ʃ/, /ʒ/, /tʃ/, /dʒ/

   buses /'bʌsɪz/　noses /'nəʊzɪz/　watches /'wɒtʃɪz/

4. Exception: house /haʊs/ → houses /'haʊzɪz/

Articles

A and *an*; pronunciation of *the*

We use *an* before vowels (*a, e, i, o, u*).

an artist   an engineer   an apple   an orange

We use *a* before consonants.

a doctor   a housewife   a banana   a tomato

Before vowels, *the* is pronounced /ði/.

the egg /ði ˈeg/   the Italians /ði ɪˈtælɪənz/

Before consonants, *the* is pronounced /ðə/.

the book /ðə ˈbʊk/   the problem /ðə ˈprɒbləm/

A/an and *the*

We use *the* when the listener *knows which one* we are talking about.

Do you mind if I open **the window**? (*The listener knows* **which window**.)
Who's **the girl** in the red dress? (*I tell the listener* **which girl** *I mean*.)
We've got a cat and a dog. **The dog**'s name is Pete. (*The listener knows* **which dog** *I mean, because of the sentence before.*)

We use *a/an* when we mean 'any one', 'it doesn't matter which one', or when the listener doesn't know which one.

I'd like to have **a dog**.
She lives in **a small flat** somewhere in Paris.

And we use *a/an* when we give the class or group that somebody/something is in.

'What do you do?'   'I'm **a student**.' (I'm student.)
'What's that?'   'It's **a camera**.'

We also use *a/an* to mean 'every' in prices and measurements.

eighty pence **a kilo**   fifty kilometres **an hour**

Expressions without articles

at home (at the home)   go home (go to home)   in bed   at school   at work

Countable and uncountable nouns

The difference between countable and uncountable nouns

Countable nouns are the names of things that you can count. (For example: *a car*, *one problem*, *two trees*, *four hundred pounds*.) We can use *a/an* with countable nouns (*a/an* means 'one'). Countable nouns have plurals.

Uncountable nouns are the names of things that you can't count. (For example: *milk*, *air*, *music*: you can't normally say *two milks* or *four musics*.)
Normally, we can't use *a/an* with uncountable nouns, and they have no plurals. Compare:

Would you like **a sandwich**?
Would you like **some** milk? (Would you like a milk?)

I like **those books**.
I like **that music**. (. . . those musics.)

Generalisations: not using *the*

When we talk about things in general (for example: *all oranges*, or *all music*), we do not use *the* with plurals or uncountables.

Oranges were expensive when I was young. (The oranges . . .)
I like **music**. (I like the music.)

We use *the* to talk about *particular things that the listener knows about*.

'Could you pass **the oranges**?'   'Here you are.'

Some problems with countables, uncountables, singulars and plurals

The following words are uncountable. We do not use them with *a/an*, and they have no plurals: *advice, information, hair, bread, news, weather, English* (and the names of other languages), *medicine, flu, toothache* (but *headache* is countable).

Could you give me **some information**?
   (. . . an information   . . . some informations)
I'd like to give you **a piece of advice**. (. . . an advice.)
What colour is her **hair**?
Here is the **news**.
We're having terrible **weather**. (. . . a terrible weather.)
She speaks very good **English**. (. . . a very good English.)
I've got **toothache**. (*BUT* I've got **a headache**.)

Words like *pound, dollar, franc, yen, peseta* are countable, but the word *money* is uncountable.

It costs eight **francs**.
It costs a lot of **money**. (. . . a lot of moneys.)

Trousers, jeans, pyjamas, pants etc. are plural. So are *glasses* and *stairs*.

Those **trousers** are too big for you.
I need **some new jeans**. (. . . a new jean.)
I wear **glasses** for reading.
It's up the **stairs** on the right. (. . . the stair . . .)

A/an and *some/any*

We only use *a/an* with singular countable nouns. With plural and uncountable nouns *a/an* is not possible. We often use *some* and *any* (see below).

There's **a woman** at the reception desk.
There are **some books** on the table.
There's **some milk** in the fridge. (There's a milk . . .)

Pronouns, determiners and question words

Subject and object pronouns and possessives

SUBJECT	OBJECT	POSSESSIVE
I	me	my
you	you	your
he	him	his
she	her	her
it	it	its
we	us	our
you	you	your
they	them	their

He likes **me**, but I don't like **him**.
They've invited **us** to a party.
Could **you** give **me** some water?
That's **my** bicycle over there. (~~. . . the my bicycle . . .~~)
Ann and **her** husband work in Stoke. (~~. . . his husband . . .~~)
John and **his** wife both play tennis. (~~. . . her wife . . .~~)

Possessive 's

Singular: -'s
Plural: -s'
Sam is **Judy's** boyfriend. (~~. . . the Judy's boyfriend.~~)
Susan's surname is Perkins. (~~Surname's Susan . . .~~)
That's my **parents'** house.

Pronunciation of possessive 's

Judy's Mary's Joe's Harry's (/z/)
Sam's Bob's Anne's Susan's (/z/)
Eric's Margaret's Jeff's Kate's (/s/)
Alice's Joyce's George's Des's (/ɪz/)

Some, any and no

Some and any

We usually use *some* in affirmative ('yes') sentences, and *any* in questions and negative ('no') sentences.

AFFIRMATIVE	QUESTION	NEGATIVE
There's **some** bread.	Is there **any** bread?	There isn't **any** bread.
I've got **some** eggs.	Have you got **any** eggs?	I haven't got **any** eggs.

Some in questions

When we offer things or ask for things, we usually use *some* in questions.

Would you like **some** coffee?
Could you lend me **some** sugar?

No (= not any)

I'm sorry, there's **no more** roast beef. (= . . . there isn't any more . . .)

(NOTE: *No* and *not any* are negative, but *any* is not negative.)

I've got **no** friends = I **haven't** got **any** friends.
(NOT ~~I've got any friends.~~)

Somebody, anything etc.

somebody	anybody	everybody	nobody
something	anything	everything	nothing
somewhere	anywhere	everywhere	nowhere

Somebody telephoned when you were out.
Would you like **something** to drink?
Have you got **anything** to read?
Have you seen my glasses **anywhere**?
I didn't understand **anything**.
Everybody was late.
She gave **everything** to her children.
'What are you doing?' '**Nothing**.'

Everybody, *everything*, *nobody* and *nothing* are singular.

Is everything all right? (~~Are everything . . . ?~~)
Everybody knows him.
Nobody likes him.

This, that, these and *those*

This cheese is terrible.
These tomatoes are very nice.
How much is **that** sweater over there?
I like **those** ear-rings that she's wearing.

Quantifiers with uncountables and plurals

WITH UNCOUNTABLES	WITH PLURALS
(not) much	(not) many
how much?	how many?
too much	too many
more	more
enough	enough
a lot of	a lot of

There isn't **much** rain here in the summer.
Are there **many** hotels in the town?

How much money do you want?
How many states are there in the USA?

I've got **too much** work.
You've given me **too many** chips.

Could I have a little **more** bread?
I'm afraid there are no **more** potatoes.

Have you got **enough** bread?
There aren't **enough** buses from our village.

The children are making **a lot of** noise.
She's got **a lot of** problems.

We can also use these words and expressions without nouns.

How much does it cost?
'Do you like her?' 'Not **much**.'
I think about you **a lot**. (~~. . . a lot of.~~)

We use *much* and *many* mostly in questions and negative sentences. In affirmative sentences, we more often use *a lot (of)*. Compare:

Have you got **many** friends?
I haven't got **many** friends.
She's got **a lot of** friends.

Question words

Who

'**Who**'s that?' 'It's my brother.' ('~~He's my brother.~~')
Who wrote *Gone with the Wind*? (~~Who did write . . .~~)
Who are you looking at? (~~Who you are . . .~~)

Which

'**Which** platform for the 3.49 train?' 'Platform 6.'
Which of these singers was not a member of the
  Beatles? (~~Who of these . . .~~)

What

'**What**'s your name?' 'Miriam Jackson.'
What does *coat* mean? (~~What means coat?~~)
What time does the next train leave? (*NOT usually* At what
  time . . .)
What sort of music do you like?
'**What** do you do?' 'I'm a student.' ('~~I'm student.~~')
What a nice colour! (~~What nice colour!~~)

How

'My name's Ann Carter.' '**How** do you do?' '**How** do you
  do?'
'**How** are you?' 'Very well, thank you. And you?'
'**How** old are you?' 'I'm 35.'
How did Louis Blériot travel from France to England?
  (~~How travelled Louis . . .~~)

Where

'**Where**'s my pen?' 'Under your book.'
'**Where** are you from?' 'Egypt.'
Where was Jesus Christ born? (~~Where was born Jesus Christ?~~)

When

When did the Second World War start? (~~When started . . .~~)

Why

'**Why** did you come to Australia?' 'To learn English.'
  (~~For learn English.~~)

Question words as subject and object

When a question word is the subject of a sentence (or with the subject of a sentence), we make questions without *do*. Compare:

Who (*subject*) **wrote** the James Bond novels?
  (~~Who did write . . .~~)
Who (*object*) **do** you like in the class?
What (*subject*) **made** that noise? (~~What did make . . .~~)
What (*object*) **do** you want?

What animals (*subject*) **live** in trees? (~~. . . do live . . .~~)
What animals (*object*) **did** Hannibal take across the Alps?
  (~~What animals took Hannibal . . .~~)

How many children (*subject*) **came** to the party?
  (~~. . . did come . . .~~)
How many children (*object*) **did** you invite to the party?

Adjectives

Position of adjectives

Before nouns
Mary has got **green** eyes. (~~... greens eyes.~~)
Sheila has got **long dark** hair.

After *be*
John is quite **nice**.
My daughters are very **tall**. (~~... are very talls.~~)

Comparative and superlative adjectives

ONE-SYLLABLE ADJECTIVES			
	Adjective	*Comparative*	*Superlative*
MOST ONE-SYLLABLE ADJECTIVES:	old	older	oldest
	short	shorter	shortest
	cheap	cheaper	cheapest
	young	younger (/ˈjʌŋgə(r)/)	youngest (/ˈjʌŋgɪst/)
	long	longer (/ˈlɒŋgə(r)/)	longest (/ˈlɒŋgɪst/)
ENDING IN -*e*:	late	later	latest
	fine	finer	finest
ENDING IN ONE VOWEL + ONE CONSONANT:	fat	fatter	fattest
	slim	slimmer	slimmest
	big	bigger	biggest
IRREGULAR:	good	better	best
	bad	worse	worst
	far	farther	farthest

TWO-SYLLABLE ADJECTIVES			
	Adjective	*Comparative*	*Superlative*
ENDING IN -*y*:	happy	happier	happiest
	easy	easier	easiest
MOST OTHERS:	complete	**more** complete	**most** complete
	famous	**more** famous	**most** famous

LONGER ADJECTIVES			
	Adjective	*Comparative*	*Superlative*
	interesting	**more** interesting	**most** interesting
	beautiful	**more** beautiful	**most** beautiful
	difficult	**more** difficult	**most** difficult

Using comparatives and superlatives

Comparatives
I'm **taller than** my mother.
I'm **much** taller than my brother.
She's **a bit** more intelligent than me.

Superlatives
Who's **the oldest** person here?
I'm **the tallest** in my family.
It's **the most beautiful** place in the world.
  (~~... of the world.~~)

(*Not*) as . . . as

I'm **as good-looking as** a film star.
He's **not as tall as** me.
A Volkswagen is not **as quiet as** a Rolls-Royce.

As and *than*

faster **than** (~~faster as~~)
more beautiful **than**
as fast **as** (~~as fast than~~)

Note also:
the same **as**
different **from**

Adverbs

Adjectives and adverbs

We use adjectives before nouns and after *be*.
We use adverbs to give more information about verbs and adjectives.
Compare:

You've got a **nice face**. (*adjective*)
You **sing nicely**. (*adverb*)

I'm **angry** with you. (*adjective*)
She **spoke angrily**. (*adverb*)

It's **terrible**. (*adjective*)
It's **terribly** cold. (*adverb*)

You speak **good** English. (*adjective*)
You **speak** English **well**. (*adverb*) (~~You speak English good.~~)

Spelling of *-ly* adverbs

	ADJECTIVE	ADVERB
MOST WORDS:	kind	kindly
	careful	carefully
		(~~carefuly~~)
	extreme	extremely
		(~~extremly~~)
ADJECTIVES ENDING IN *-y*:	happy	happily
	angry	angrily
ADJECTIVES ENDING IN *-ble*:	comfortable	comfortably

Position of adverbs

Don't put adverbs between the verb and the object.

She speaks English **well**. (~~She speaks well English.~~)
I opened the letter **carefully**. (~~I opened carefully the letter.~~)
I **never** read science fiction. (~~I read never science fiction.~~)

Frequency adverbs: use and position

How **often** do you go to the cinema?
Do you **ever** go to the opera?

I	always	come here on Sunday mornings.
	very often	
	quite often	
	sometimes	
	occasionally	
	hardly ever	
	never	

(NOTE: These adverbs come after *am/are/is/was/were* – e.g. I *am always* late.)

I come here	every day.
	every three days.
	once a day.
	twice a week.
	three times a year.

Adverbs of degree

I'm	not at all	tired.
	not very	
	a bit	
	quite	
	very	
	extremely	

Comparative and superlative adverbs

We usually make comparative and superlative adverbs with *more* and *most*.

Could you speak **more slowly**?
She sings **most beautifully**.

Exceptions: *faster, fastest; better, best.*

She can run **faster** than me.
I speak English **better** than my father.

Prepositions

Talking about time

I'll see you **at** ten o'clock.
     on Thursday.
     on June 22nd.
     at the weekend.
     in the morning.
I don't work **on** Saturdays.

I'll see you **in** three days. (= three days from now)

We go skiing every year **for** two weeks.
I've been here **for** six weeks.
     since Christmas.

I work **from** nine **to/until** six.

She only studies **before** exams.
I'm free **after** six o'clock.

half **past** nine
five **to** ten

No preposition

What time do you get up? (*NOT usually* At what time . . . ?)
I'll see you **this afternoon**.
I'll see you **next week**.
I saw her **last week**.

Talking about place

on / under / in / near

It's **on** the table (~~. . . in the table.~~)
  under your chair.
  in the fridge.
  near the door.

in the living room
in a small flat
on the second floor
at 53 Park Street

in Park Street
in London
in England

He **lived in** Saigon.
He **studied at** Saigon University.

I'm going **to** Edinburgh tomorrow. (~~. . . going at . . .~~)
I'll **arrive at** Waverley Station at 9.15. (~~. . . arrive to . . .~~)

She was the first woman to fly **across** the Atlantic.
                              round the world.

'Where are you **from**?'   'I'm **from** Ireland.'

He's **at** the disco.
  at the supermarket.
  at the doctor's.
  at the bus stop.
  at the station.
  at home.
  at work.
  at school.
  at lunch.
  in bed.
  on his way to work.

It's **by** the reception desk.
  near the stairs.
  next to the post office.
  opposite the station.
  outside the window.
  behind the tree.
  in front of the tree.
  between those two trees.

Go straight **on for** 300 metres and it's **on** the right.

Our bedroom is **over** the living room.

He got **into** his car and drove away.
She got **out of** the car and went **into** the house.

No preposition
I want to go **home**. (~~. . . to home.~~)

Other uses of prepositions

Here's a letter **for** you.

the girl **in** jeans
the man **with** a beard
My sister looks **like** me.

We're all slim **except** Joe.

'How old is she?'   '**Over** twenty.'
                    '**Under** thirty.'

good **at** maths
good **at** running

the highest mountain **in** the world

We went to Spain **on** holiday.
We went there **by** bus/car/train/air.

I often think **about** you.
We were talking **about** money.

I can't go **without** sleep for very long.

Look at my new dress.
Would you like to **listen to** some music?
I'm **looking for** a sweater.

Putting things together

Joining subjects

Both Al **and** Jake robbed a bank.   **Neither** Al **nor** Jake went to bed early.

Conjunctions: building sentences

And and *but*
The British sailors woke up **and** started fighting, **but** they could not stop Jones and his men.

That
One American captain wanted to show the British **that** size was not everything.
We both agree **that** I'm more optimistic than her.
He told the policeman (**that**) he got up at eight o'clock.
  (~~He told that he got up . . .~~)
He said (**that**) they went to an art gallery.
  (~~He said the policeman that . . .~~)

Who
Galileo was the man **who** discovered sunspots.
They laughed at the small navy of the Americans, **who** were fighting to be free of Britain.

Where
The Americans left Whitehaven and sailed to Scotland, **where** they carried out more attacks.

When
When Fred's hungry he goes to a restaurant.

As soon as
As soon as he arrived, he took a group of his men to an inn.

Because
Amelia Earhart stopped studying **because** she wanted to learn to fly.

Before and *after*
Always warm up **before** you run.
Rest for a few minutes **after** you finish.

If
If you press button F, you'll get a cup of coffee.
  (~~If you will press . . .~~)
If I have time, I'll come and see you. (~~If I will have time . . .~~)

Joining sentences

Then they started work. **First of all** they went to the fort and destroyed the guns.
Next, they began burning British ships . . . **Finally,** the Americans left Whitehaven . . .

Problems with some words

Verbs with two objects

Some verbs (for example *bring*, *give*, *lend*, *show*, *tell*) often have two objects.

Could you bring **me some water**?
Can I give **you a little more coffee**?
Could you lend **me some sugar**?
Could you show **me some black sweaters**, please?
I told **her my address**.

Lend and *borrow*

Lend is like *give*; *borrow* is like *take*.

Could you **lend** me some sugar?
Could I **borrow** some sugar (from you)?
(Could I borrow you some sugar?)

Like and *would like*

Like means 'enjoy'; *would like* means 'want'.

'Do you **like** dancing?' 'Yes, I do. I go dancing every weekend.'
'**Would** you **like** to dance?' 'No, thanks. I'm tired.'

Be like, look like, and *look*

'What **is** she **like**?' ('How is she?') 'She's a bit shy, but very nice.'

He **looks like** a footballer.
I think he **looks** more **like** a businessman.
She **looks like** her mother.

She **looks** bad-tempered.
You **look** tired.

Get

1. *Get* + object = 'obtain', 'receive', 'fetch'.

   Where can I **get** some stamps?
   I **get** a letter from my mother every week.
   Can you **get** me some bread, please?

2. *Get* + adjective = 'become'.

   It's **getting** late.
   If you work too hard you'll **get** tired.

3. *Get* + adverb particle / preposition = 'move'.

   What time do you usually **get up**?
   It takes me an hour to **get to** work.
   Get on the bus outside the station, and **get off** at Park Street.
   Get out!!

4. *Have got* = 'have', 'possess'.

   You've **got** beautiful eyes.

5. *Get lost, married, killed* = 'be lost, married *etc.*'

   We went for a walk and **got lost** in the woods.
   She's **getting married** next week.
   He **got killed** in a car crash.

Born

I **was born** in 1936. (I am born . . .)
When **were** you **born**?

Agree

I agree. (I am agree.)
He doesn't agree.

Conversational grammar

Showing interest: reply questions

'I'm Pisces.' '**Are** you?'
'I've got a cold.' 'Oh, **have** you?'
'My father **can** speak five languages.' '**Can** he?'
'I love skiing.' '**Do** you?'
'I **slept** badly last night.' 'Oh, **did** you?'

So am I etc.

'I'm tired.' '**So am I**.' '**I'm not**.'
'I've got a pink Rolls-Royce.' '**So have I**.' '**I haven't**.'
'Mary can swim.' '**So can Alice**.' '**Louise can't**.'
'I go skiing twice a year.' '**So do I**.' '**I don't**.'
'John phoned last night.' '**So did your mother**.'

Doing things in English

Meeting and greeting

Introductions: meeting for the first time
'Joe, this is Pat.' 'How do you do?' 'How do you do?'

Formal greetings
Good morning/afternoon/evening.
Goodbye / Good night.

Informal greetings
Hi/Hello.
Bye / Goodbye / See you / Good night.

Asking about health
'How are you?' 'Very well, thanks.'
                'Fine, thanks. And you?'
                'Not too bad.'

Asking for personal information

'Where are you from?' 'Scotland.'
'Where do you live?' 'In Edinburgh.'
'Where do you work?' 'In a small shop in George Street.'
'What's your phone number?' '7623305.' (Seven six two, double three oh five.)
'What newspaper do you read?' *The Independent.*
'How do you travel to work?' 'By bus.'
'What sort of books do you like?' 'Science fiction.'
'Are you interested in politics?' 'Yes, I am.'

Opinions, likes and dislikes

'How do you like this place?' 'Great / Not bad / Not much / Terrible.'
Do you like modern jazz?
What do you think of the government?
What's your favourite food?

I like the Greek statue **very much.**
I **quite** like the mask.
It's **OK.**
I like the Vermeer **best.**
I **hate** shopping.
I don't like classical music **at all.**
'Do you like travelling?' '**It depends.**'

Apologising

'**Excuse me**, is your name Fred Andrews?'
'No, **I'm sorry**, it's not. It's Jake Barker.'
'**Pardon?**'
'It's Jake Barker.'
'Oh, **I'm sorry.**'
'**That's all right.**'

Talking about feelings

I feel ill.
What's the matter?
My eyes hurt.   My arm hurts.
Do they hurt / Does it hurt very badly?
I've got a (bad) cold / a (bad) headache / (bad) toothache / flu / a temperature. (*American*: a toothache; the flu)
Why don't you see the doctor/dentist?

Suggesting; inviting; answering invitations

'Are you doing anything this evening? **Would you like** to see a film?'
'**I don't know**, I'm a bit tired. **I don't really want** to go out tonight.'
'Well, **what about** tomorrow?'
'**I'd love to**, but **I'm afraid** I'm not free. I'm going to a concert in London.'
'**Let's** do something at the weekend. Are you free?'
'**Perhaps.** Yes, **why not?**'
'**How about** Saturday? **Shall we** have dinner?'
'**What a** nice idea!'
'OK. **See you** about eight o'clock.'
'Right, see you then.'

Asking for and giving permission

Do you mind if I	sit here?
	open the window?
	smoke?
	look at your paper?

Not at all.
No, please do.
Go ahead.

I'm sorry, it's not free.
Well, it's a bit cold.
Well, I'd rather you didn't.
Well, I'm reading it myself, actually.

Lending and borrowing

I'm sorry to trouble you, but could you lend me some sugar?
Could you possibly lend me your car?
Could I borrow your keys **for a moment**?

Yes, **here you are.**
Yes, **of course.**

I'm sorry, **I need it/them.**
I'm afraid I haven't got one/any.
I'm sorry, **I'm afraid** I can't.

Telling people to do things

Please hurry!
Take your time.
Don't worry.
Look.
Come in.
Wait here, please.
Be careful.
Follow me, please.
Look out!

Ordering and asking

I'll start with soup, please, and then **I'll have** roast beef.
Chicken **for me**, please.
Could you bring me a beer?
Just some water, please.
a little more coffee
Could you bring us **the bill**, please?
Is service **included**?

Shopping

'Can I help you?'   'I'm just looking.'
'I'm looking for a sweater.'   'Here's a lovely one.'
What a lovely sweater! (~~What lovely sweater!~~)
What nice shoes!
Those aren't very nice.   I don't like that very much.
Can I look round?
Can I try them on?
'Have you got anything in black?'   'I'll just see.'
'No, I'm afraid I haven't. Would you like to try these?'
   (~~Would you like try these?~~)
How much are they?   How much is it?
I'll take them, please.
I'd like a red one.
I'd like to look at some watches.
   (~~I'd like look at some watches.~~)

Asking for and giving directions

Excuse me. Where's the nearest post office, please?
Excuse me. Is there a post office near here, please?

It's over there by the police station.
First on the right, then second on the left.
Take the first right, second left, then straight on.

How far is it?

About a hundred metres.
About a hundred yards.

Thank you very much.
Not at all.

I'm sorry. I don't know.
Thank you anyway.

Telephoning

Can/Could I speak to . . . ?
This is . . .
Is that . . . ?
He/She's not in.
Can I take a message?

Asking about English

What's this?   What's this called in English, please?
What are these?
Is this a pen or a pencil?   Is this a lighter?
How do you say *arroyo* in English?
What does *shy* mean? (~~What means *shy*?~~)
How do you pronounce k–n–e–w?
How do you spell that word?
Could you speak more slowly, please?

Talking about ages, heights and weights

The Great Pyramid **is** 4,500 years **old**.
It **is** 135 metres **high**.
The car **is** 4 metres **long**.
The statue **weighs** three kilos.

Lucy **is** four months **old**.
Her mother **is** 40 (years old).
I **am** 1 metre 91.
I **weigh** 85 kilos.

She's **over** 21 and **under** 30.

How old/tall are you?
How much do you weigh?

Dates

WRITE	SAY
14 Jan(uary) 1990 14.1.90 (GB) 1.14.90 (US)	January the fourteenth, nineteen ninety (GB) January fourteenth . . . (US)
5 Apr(il) 1892	April the fifth, eighteen ninety-two
9 Dec(ember) 1600	December the ninth, sixteen hundred
14 May 1906	May the fourteenth, nineteen hundred and six OR: . . . nineteen oh six

Writing formal letters

> Flat 6
> Monument House
> Castle Street
> Newcastle NE1 2HH
>
> 12 September 1990
>
> Dear Mr Bell,
>
> I am arriving at Waverley Station, Edinburgh . . .
>
> . . .
>
> I look forward to seeing you.
>
> Yours sincerely,
>
> Paul Sanders

Solutions to crosswords and problems

Lesson 1B

5

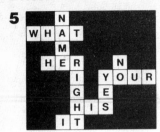

Lesson 1D

6

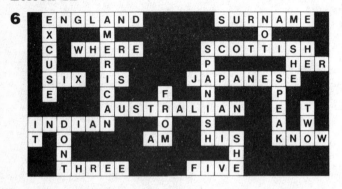

Lesson 3D

6

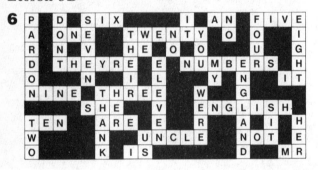

Lesson 4A

6

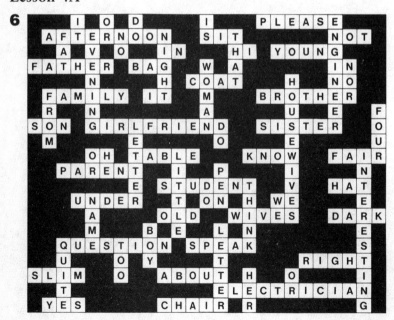

Lesson 4C

6 There are two doctors, and only one of the children is a doctor, so one of the parents is a doctor. The two doctors are fair, and the father and the daughter are dark; so the mother, Mary, is a doctor. Elizabeth is the only daughter, so she is the actress. Tom is an architect, so he isn't one of the children: he's the father. Harry is dark, so he isn't a doctor, he's an artist. John is a doctor.

Lesson 5B

4 If the photographer and the doctor are women, the architect is a man. If Philip is not an artist, he is an architect; and he lives on the ground floor. Jane lives on the first floor, and Susan is not a doctor, so Jane is a doctor. If Jane is a doctor, Susan is a photographer. If Susan lives under Dan, she lives on the second floor, and Dan lives on the third floor (he is an artist).

NAME	JOB	FLOOR
Dan	artist	third
Susan	photographer	second
Jane	doctor	first
Philip	architect	ground

Lesson 5C

3 1. True (between Alaska and Siberia).
2. False (but in 1610 it was true).
3. False (4,807 metres).
4. False (100 pence).
5. True.
6. False (1.6 kilometres).
7. True.
8. False (there are penguins in the Antarctic).

Lesson 6A

4 Peter likes Anne. John likes two people; one of them can't be Catherine, because only one person likes her, and that is Anne. So John likes Anne and Peter, and the person who doesn't like Anne is Catherine.

Lesson 6B

5

Lesson 7A

7 980 calories.

Lesson 7B

6 girl's bicycle: £40
winter coat: £20
12lbs of apples: £1
two Alsatian puppies: £90
Renault 12TL: £650
violin: £125
three ducks: £5.25

Total cost: £931.25

Lesson 8A

6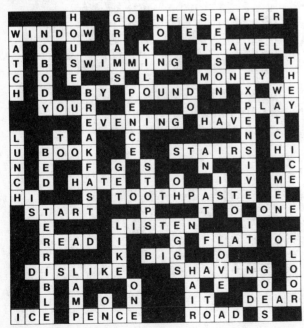

Lesson 10A

5

Lesson 12A

7

Lesson 13B

5 Valerie is not the organist, so put *no* in that column.

Lorna cannot speak German, so put *no* in that column.

Mary cannot speak Italian, so put *no* in that column.

Anthea cannot play the violin, so put *no* in that column.

Anthea cannot speak Spanish, so put *no* in that column.

Valerie can't speak French, so put *no* in that column.

Lorna doesn't play the harp, so put *no* in that column.

The girl who plays the violin speaks French, so Valerie (who doesn't speak French) cannot play the violin. Put *no* in that column.

This puts three *no*s in the violin column; so Lorna is the one who can play the violin, and since the girl who plays the violin speaks French, that is Lorna, too. Put *yes* in those two columns and *no* in all Lorna's other columns.

This puts three *no*s in the organ column. Put *yes* in Anthea's organ column and *no* in her other instrument columns.

The organist can't speak Italian, so put *no* in Anthea's Italian column.

This leaves Valerie who can speak Italian; put *yes* there and *no* in the other language columns.

This means Mary can speak Spanish; which means Anthea can speak German.

The only harp column now free is Valerie's. Valerie can speak Italian and play the harp.

Lesson 13C

4 – The highest mountain in the world is K2, not Everest.
– The smallest continent in the world is Australia.
– The largest ocean in the world is the Pacific.
– The largest sea in the world is the South China Sea.
– The farthest spot from land in the world is in the South Pacific.
– The longest river in the world is the Nile or the Amazon. (It depends on how you measure.)
– The highest lake in the world is Titicaca, in Peru.
– The largest active volcano in the world is Mauna Loa in Hawaii.

Lesson 14A

6

Lesson 15C

5 A: Manchester are playing against Arsenal on the 12th and Tottenham on the 19th. So on the 26th Manchester are playing against Liverpool, which means that Arsenal are playing against Tottenham.

B: O'Connor is performing on September 19th or 21st before he leaves Fantasia, which means that he is either doing folk songs in the Jazz Cellar or acting *Hamlet*. But Ducarme is the actor, so Ducarme is doing *Hamlet*, and O'Connor is doing the folk songs. Haas is talking about butterflies (he isn't musical); so Carlotti is playing the violin.

Lesson 16A

6

Lesson 17B

6

132

Lesson 18C

6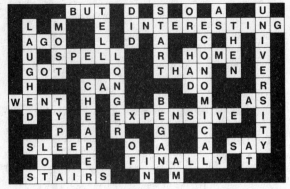

Lesson 24A

5

```
AT   NORTH   O
SO   ON  H   IN
     A C   EAT
WINTER   USE
E    I   AT  A
SUMMER   U   S
T    E       MET
     W   SPRING
DIE          S  GO
ON   SOUTH   F
```

Lesson 20B

5

```
FUNNY    IT   C
A   O E      W    A
V   I S   POOR
O   S TOO    R
UNIVERSITY
R   E R      S    R
I     RED    ICAN
T         A  B    I
EARLY     LEND
    T        MY   SO
```

Lesson 21B

2 Louise is going to be the lorry driver because her job begins with the same letter as her name. Kate is going to be the tennis player because she is not going to study after leaving school. Mark is going to be the teacher since he is not going to be the doctor or the engineer. This means that George is going to be the doctor since he cannot become the teacher. Phil is going to be the engineer.

Lesson 22C

7

Acknowledgements

The authors and publishers are grateful to the following copyright owners for permission to reproduce photographs, illustrations, texts and music. Every endeavour has been made to contact copyright owners and apologies are expressed for any omissions.

page 5: Reproduced by permission of *Punch*.   page 6: Reproduced by permission of *Punch*.   page 10: *b* From *Weekend Book of Jokes 22* courtesy of Weekend.   page 14: *b* Reproduced by permission of *Punch*.   page 23: From *Weekend Book of Jokes 22* courtesy of Weekend.   page 24: *b* Reproduced by permission of British Telecom. ® The British Telecom logo is a registered trademark of British Telecommunications public limited company.   page 25: *b* Reproduced by permission of *Punch*.   page 26: From *Weekend Book of Jokes 22* courtesy of Weekend.   page 31: Chart from THE F-PLAN CALORIE AND FIBRE CHART by Audrey Eyton (Penguin Books 1982), copyright © Audrey Eyton, 1982, pp 76–7.   page 37: *t* Reproduced by permission of the IFL Penfriend Service; *br* Reproduced by permission of The Post Office (International Letters) and Union Postale Universelle (Bureau International).   page 38: Reproduced by permission of *Punch*.   page 39: Reproduced by permission of *Punch*.   page 40: Reprinted by permission of Johnny Hart and Creators Syndicate, Inc.   page 43: *bl* Reproduced by permission of *Punch*.   page 47: Courtesy of Hilton International, London.   page 49: Reproduced by permission of *Punch*.   page 50: Reproduced by permission of *Punch*.   page 53: *b* Excerpt from 'Hello, Britain' text reprinted courtesy of the British Tourist Authority; London Regional Transport trade mark by permission of the London Transport Museum; British Rail logo by permission of the British Railways Board.   page 59: Reproduced by permission of Dover Publications, Inc., New York.   page 62: Reproduced by permission of *Punch*.   page 63: From *Weekend Book of Jokes 22* courtesy of Weekend.   page 65: Reprinted by permission of The Putnam Publishing Group from THE SPY WHO CAME IN FROM THE COLD by John Le Carré. Copyright © 1963 by Victor Gollancz. Also by permission of David Higham Associates Ltd and Le Carré Productions.   page 66: From *The Guinness Book of Records* © Guinness Publications Ltd by permission of Guinness Publishing Ltd.   page 68: © Express Newspapers plc.   page 69: *bl* and *br* Reproduced by permission of *Punch*.   page 72: Reproduced by permission of *Punch*.   page 77: *t* From *Adolescent Boys of East London* by Peter Wilmott, reprinted by permission of Routledge & Kegan Paul; *bl* and *br* Reproduced by permission of *Punch*.   page 79: *bl* and *br* Reproduced by permission of *Punch*.   page 86: *b* Reproduced by permission of *Punch*.   page 87: Adapted from *Love and War in the Apennines* by Eric Newby, reprinted by permission of Collins.   page 88: Cartoon by SAX reproduced by permission of Mail Newspapers plc.   page 89: Reproduced by permission of *Punch*.   page 90: *b* From *Weekend Book of Jokes 22* courtesy of Weekend.   page 92: *tl* Adapted from *How to be an Alien* by George Mikes © André Deutsch 1984; *tr* Cartoon by Artemas Cole (Manuel Gonzalez); *br* Reproduced by permission of *Reveille* and Syndication International (1986) Ltd.   page 97: *r* From *Weekend Book of Jokes 23* courtesy of Weekend.   page 98: *b* Reproduced by permission of *Punch*.   page 99: Adapted from *Baby and Child Care*. Copyright © 1945, 1946, © 1957, 1968, 1976 by Dr Benjamin Spock. Reprinted by permission of Pocket Books, a division of Simon & Schuster, Inc.   page 100: *tr* From PHYSICAL FITNESS developed by the Royal Canadian Air Force (Penguin Books, 1964), Crown copyright © Queen's Printer, Canada, 1958, 1960: reprinted by permission of the Ministry of Supply and Services, Canada, Penguin Books Ltd, UK, and the Government Printing Office, New Zealand; *bl* and *br* Reproduced by permission of *Punch*.   page 105: Abridged from *The Guinness Book of Answers* © Guinness Superlatives Ltd and Norris McWhirter, by permission of Guinness Publishing Ltd.   page 106: *t* Reproduced by permission of the Consumers' Association; *cl* and *br* Reproduced by permission of *Punch*.   page 108: Courtesy of Rolls-Royce Motor Cars Ltd.

Artist Partners: Tony Graham, pages 13, 21 *r*, 37 *bl*, 42 *b*; Robin Harris, page 99; Biz Hull, page 11 *l*. B. L. Kearley: Tony Kenyon, pages 4 *b*, 5, 7 *r*, 8 *b*, 9 *b*, 11 *tr*,12 *b*, 14, 16 *t*, 20 *bl*, 23, 24, 25 *t*, 53, 100; Barry Wilkinson, page 74.   Maggie Mundy: Hemesh Alles, page 97 *l*; Maggie Brand, page 96 *t*; Ann Johns, pages 11 *br*, 15, 20 *t*, 25 *c*, 29 *b*, 33, 39 *b*, 44, 48, 51, 56, 57, 61, 67, 71, 75, 81, 86 *t*, 90 *t*, 94, 98 *t*, 103, 107, 110.   Young Artists: Sarah John, pages 22 *b*, 34, 52, 65.

Nancy Anderson, pages 76, 80.   John Blackman, pages 42 *t*, 58, 69 *t*, 101.   Joe McEwan, pages 18, 21 *l*, 22, 36, 38.   Rodney Sutton, pages 6, 7 *l*, 8, 10 *t*, 12 *t*, 16 *b*, 27, 30, 32, 39 *t*, 43 *r*, 45, 55 *t*, 66, 96 *b*.

Darren Marsh, pages 4 *tc*, *c* and *cr*, 9 *t* and *c*, 29 *c*. Ken Weedon, page 47.   The Image Bank, pages 4 *tl* and *cl*, 10 *c*, 19.

(*t* = top *b* = bottom *c* = centre *r* = right *l* = left)